The Metaphysical Po...

The Metaphysical Poets

with an Introduction and Bibliography

Wordsworth Poetry Library

This edition published 1995 by Wordsworth Editions Ltd,
Cumberland House, Crib Street, Ware, Hertfordshire SG12 9ET.

Copyright © Wordsworth Editions Ltd 1995.

ISBN 1-85326-439-3

Typeset in the UK by Antony Gray.
Printed and bound in Denmark by Nørhaven.

The paper in this book is produced from pure wood
pulp, without the use of chlorine or any other substance
harmful to the environment. The energy used in its
production consists almost entirely of hydroelectricity
and heat generated from waste materials, thereby
conserving fossil fuels and contributing little to the
greenhouse effect.

INTRODUCTION

In discussing metaphysical poetry, it is important to understand just what is meant by the term. The *Shorter Oxford English Dictionary* defines the poets themselves as ' . . . certain seventeenth-century poets exhibiting subtlety of thought and complex imagery'. The poetry itself is described as 'expressing emotion within an intellectual context'.

Like all dictionary definitions, this is accurate as far as it goes. The term 'metaphysical' has a chequered history, and perhaps the first use of it in the terms which we understand today was by Fulvio Testo in contrasting the simpler imagery of classical poetry with the *concetti metafisici e ideali* of the poetry of his age. In English terminology, it was, perhaps, John Dryden who first used the term in remarking of John Donne, 'He affects the metaphysics, not only in his satires, but in his amorous verses, where nature only should reign; and perplexes the minds of the fair sex with nice speculations of philosophy, when he should engage their hearts, and entertain them with the softness of love.' Nearly a century later, Samuel Johnson, in his *Life of Cowley*, wrote, 'At the beginning of the seventeenth century appeared a race of writers that may be termed the metaphysical poets.' Neither writer approved of the school of poets or the term 'metaphysical'.

So what does it mean? The clue lies in Testo's *concetti metafisici* which indicates an ingenious turn of expression or conceit. Conceits mark the special character of the poetry, and are whimsical, ingenious and extended metaphors or similes in which an object, scene, person situation or emotion is presented in terms of a simple analogue, usually chosen from the natural world. The verse tends to avoid smooth and regular metre in order to achieve dramatic or conversational effects, and to employ unusual syntax and unconventional types of imagery chosen from philosophy, religion and theology, and from the arts, crafts sciences and the ordinary daily life of the period in which the poets lived.

Metaphysical poetry is a long way from the classical formality of the Augustan Age or the self-absorption of the Romantics. The metaphysical poets might well have felt queasy at Wordsworth's definition of poetry as ' . . . the spontaneous overflow of powerful feelings: it takes its origin from emotion recollected in tranquillity'. For them, the object of their poetry was, in the words of T. S. Eliot, to fuse reason and passion, unifying thought and feeling. So, in his many frankly sexy poems, John Donne reflects the age of geographical discovery in which he lived – for example, in 'The Good-Morrow':

> Let sea-discoverers to new worlds have gone,
> Let Maps to others, worlds on worlds have showne,
> Let us possesse one world, each hath one, and is one . . .

and in the famous lines from 'To his Mistris Going to Bed':

> Licence my roaving hands, and let them go,
> Before, behind, between, above, below.
> O my America! my new-found-land,
> My kingdome, safeliest when with one man man'd,
> My Myne of precious stones, My Emperie,
> How blest am I in this discovering thee!

In a more serious vein, Henry Vaughan, in 'The World', uses a classic conceit of extended simile:

> I saw Eternity the other night
> Like a great Ring of pure and endless light,
>   All calm, as it was bright,
> And round beneath it, Time in hours, days, years
>   Driv'n by the spheres
> Like a vast shadow mov'd, In which the world
>   And all her train were hurl'd . . .

Eternity and religion were constant subjects of the metaphysical poets, and it has to be remembered that the two most notable metaphysical poets, Donne and Herbert, were clergymen. To them, the conceit of personifying abstract concepts such as sin, love and death was the natural way of expressing their concerns. In 'Holy Sonnet XI', Donne addresses his own imperfections, comparing them with consistent denial of Christ's redemption; 'Holy Sonnet XIV' introduces a sexual element in his longing for oneness with God; and in 'Holy Sonnet X' – 'Death, be not Proud . . . ' – the taunting of death personified is a masterpiece of Christian Faith. George Herbert is altogether gentler than Donne, and did not draw on a racy youth in the way that Donne did in his earlier poems. His conceits lay more in the everyday manifestations of God in the world, and his intimate and, on occasion, chatty relationship with Him. 'Easter Wings' combines the serious concern of achieving grace in an ingenious display of virtuosity in which the poem is laid out in the form of two pairs of wings to help the poet fly to God. In 'The Pulley', God is treated as a familiar friend, endowed with great generosity as well as a sense of proportion and humour.

It is this humour, this wit, that is the other main characteristic of metaphysical poetry. The consistent use of the punch-line is one of the main delights of the poetry. It may occasionally be necessary to tease it out, but the final couplets of 'To his Mistris Going to Bed', 'To his Coy Mistress' and Shakespeare's 'Sonnet 130' are familiar to almost all poetry lovers. On a less carnal note, 'The Pulley' and 'Love' by George Herbert, 'On His Blindness' by John Milton and Henry Vaughan's 'The Retreate', so reminiscent of Traherne's devotional essays *Centuries*, all have a witty and a punchy finish.

With regard to the selection of poems in this book, many are not 'metaphysical' in the strictest academic sense of the word. However, their unifying theme is one of conceit and wit, and they are arranged chronologically so that the development of these two qualities can be seen clearly. So, in Sir Walter Raleigh's 'The Passionate Mans Pilgrimage', we see an early manifestation of the metaphor:

> Give me my Scallop shell of quiet,
> My staffe of Faith to walke upon,
> My Scrip of Joy, Immortall diet,
> My bottle of salvation . . .

as the poet imagines life as a pilgrimage to the shrine of St James at Compostella. Shakespeare's 'My mistress' eyes are nothing like the sun' is an early example of both conceit and wit in the number of similes and the final, wholehearted declaration of the concluding couplet.

A few words must be said about the spelling as well. Seventeenth-century spelling was never consistent; Shakespeare spelt his name several different ways, and if so important a word as an autograph could vary, it is hardly surprising that spelling differed from draft to draft and from poet to poet. For instance, in George Herbert's 'Love', the last couplet of the second verse reads

> Love took my hand, and smiling did reply,
>   'Who made the eyes but I?'

Early editions read

>   Who made thee eyes but I?

In the seventeenth century 'thee' could be either the definite article or the dative form of 'thou'. For many people, the second alternative is the more powerful. So, in a happily inconsistent way, this anthology presents the poems spelt so to make them readily comprehensible to the modern reader while attempting to keep a strong flavour of the originals.

FURTHER READING

Alvarez, A., *The School of Donne*, 1961

Duncan, J. E., *The Revival of Metaphysical Poetry*, 1959

Eliot, T. S., 'Metaphysical Poets', *TLS*, 20 October 1921

Sloane, M. C., *The Visual in Metaphysical Poetry*, 1982

Smith, A. J., *The Metaphysics of Love*, 1985

Tuve, R., *Elizabethan and Metaphysical Imagery*, 1947

White, H. C., *Metaphysical Poets*, 1936

CONTENTS

THE POEMS

SIR WALTER RALEIGH
(1552–1618)

The Passionate Mans Pilgrimage, supposed to be written by one at the point of death

Give me my Scallop shell of quiet,
My staffe of Faith to walke upon,
My Scrip of Joy, Immortall diet,
My bottle of salvation:
My Gowne of Glory, hopes true gage,
And thus Ile take my pilgrimage.

Blood must be my bodies balmer,
No other balme will there be given
Whilst my soule like a white Palmer
Travels to the land of heaven,
Over the silver mountaines,
Where spring the Nectar fountaines:
And there Ile kisse
The Bowle of blisse,
And drinke my eternall fill
On every milken hill.
My soule will be a-drie before,
But after, it will nere thirst more.

And by the happie blisfull way
More peacefull Pilgrims I shall see,
That have shooke off their gownes of clay,
And goe appareld fresh like mee.
Ile bring them first
To slake their thirst
And then to taste those Nectar suckets
At the cleare wells
Where sweetnes dwells,
Drawne up by Saints in Christall buckets.

And when our bottles and all we,
Are fild with immortalitie:
Then the holy paths wee'le travell
Strewde with Rubies thicke as gravell,
Ceelings of Diamonds, Saphire floores,
High walles of Corall and Pearl Bowres.

From thence to heavens Bribeles hall
Where no corrupted voyces brall,
No Conscience molten into gold,
Nor forg'd accusers bought and sold,
No cause deferd, nor vaine spent Journey,
For there Christ is the Kings Atturney:
Who pleades for all without degrees,
And he hath Angells, but no fees.

When the grand twelve million Jury
Of our sinnes with sinfull fury,
Gainst our soules blacke verdicts give,
Christ pleades his death, and then we live,
Be thou my speaker taintles pleader,
Unblotted Lawyer, true proceeder,
Thou movest salvation even for almes:
Not with a bribed Lawyers palmes.

And this is my eternall plea,
To him that made Heaven, Earth and Sea,
Seeing my flesh must die so soone,
And want a head to dine next noone,
Just at the stroke when my vaines start and spred
Set on my soule an everlasting head.
Then am I readie like a palmer fit,
To tread those blest paths which before I writ.

ANONYMOUS

Epitaph:
On Sir Walter Rawleigh
at his Execution

Great heart, who taught thee so to dye?
Death yielding thee the victory?
Where took'st thou leave of life? if there,
How couldst thou be so freed from feare?
But sure thou dy'st and quit'st the state
Of flesh and blood before thy fate.
Else what a miracle were wrought,
To triumph both in flesh and thought?
I saw in every stander by,
Pale death, life onely in thine eye:
Th' example that thou left'st was then,
We look for when thou dy'st agen.
   Farewell, truth shall thy story say,
We dy'd, thou onely liv'dst that day.

Epigram:
Fatum Supremum

All buildings are but monuments of death,
All clothes, but winding sheets for our last knell,
All dainty, fattings for the worms beneath,
All curious musique, but our passing bell;
   Thus death is nobly waited on, for why?
   All that we have is but deaths livery.

WILLIAM SHAKESPEARE
1568–1616

Sonnet 130

My mistress' eyes are nothing like the sun;
Coral is far more red than her lips red:
If snow be white, why then her breasts are dun;
If hairs be wires, black wires grow on her head.
I have seen roses damaskt, red and white,
But no such roses see I in her cheeks;
And in some perfumes is there more delight
Than in the breath that from my mistress reeks.
I love to hear her speak, yet well I know
That music hath a far more pleasing sound:
I grant I never saw a goddess go;
My mistress, when she walks, treads on the ground.
   And yet, by heaven, I think my love as rare
   As any she belied with false compare.

SIR HENRY WOTTON
1568–1639

A Hymn to my God in a night of my late Sicknesse

Oh thou great Power, in whom I move,
For whom I live, to whom I die,
Behold me through thy beams of love,
Whilst on this couch of tears I lye;
  And Cleanse my sordid soul within,
  By thy Christs Blood, the bath of sin.

No hallowed Oyls, no grains I need,
No rags of Saints, no purging fire,
One rosie drop from David's Seed
Was worlds of Seas, to quench thine Ire.
  O precious Ransome! which once paid,
  That *Consummatum est* was said.

And said by him, that said no more,
But seal'd it with his sacred Breath.
Thou then, that hast dispung'd my score,
And dying, wast the death of Death;
  Be to me now, on thee I call,
  My Life, my Strength, my Joy, my All.

Upon the sudden Restraint of the Earl of Somerset, then falling from favour

Dazzled thus with height of place,
Whilst our Hopes our wits Beguile,
No man marks the narrow space
'Twixt a Prison and a Smile.

Then since Fortunes favours fade,
You that in her arms do sleep,
Learn to swim and not to wade;
For the Hearts of Kings are deep.

But if Greatness be so blind,
As to trust in Towers of Air,
Let it be with Goodness lin'd,
That at least the Fall be fair.

Then though darkened you shall say,
When Friends fail and Princes frown,
Vertue is the roughest way,
But proves at night a *Bed of Down*.

JOHN DONNE
1572–1631

His Picture

Here take my Picture; though I bid farewell,
Thine, in my heart, where my soule dwels, shall dwell.
'Tis like me now, but I dead, 'twill be more
When wee are shadowes both, then 'twas before.
When weather-beaten I come backe; my hand,
Perhaps with rude oares torne, or Sun beams tann'd,
My face and brest of haircloth, and my head
With cares rash sodaine stormes, being o'rspread,
My body'a sack of bones, broken within,
And powders blew staines scatter'd on my skinne;
If rivall fooles taxe thee to'have lov'd a man,
So foule, and course, as, Oh, I may seeme than,
This shall say what I was: and thou shalt say,
Doe his hurts reach mee? doth my worth decay?
Or doe they reach his judging minde, that hee
Should now love lesse, what hee did love to see?
That which in him was faire and delicate,
Was but the milke, which in loves childish state
Did nurse it: who now is growne strong enough
To feed on that, which to disused tasts seemes tough.

On his Mistris

By our first strange and fatall interview,
By all desires which thereof did ensue,
By our long starving hopes, by that remorse
Which my words masculine perswasive force
Begot in thee, and by the memory
Of hurts, which spies and rivals threatned me,
I calmly beg: But by thy fathers wrath,
By all paines, which want and divorcement hath,
I conjure thee, and all the oathes which I

And thou have sworne to seale joynt constancy,
Here I unsweare, and overswear them thus,
Thou shalt not love by wayes so dangerous.
Temper, oh faire Love, loves impetuous rage,
Be my true Mistris still, not my faign'd Page;
I'll goe, and, by thy kinde leave, leave behinde
Thee, onely worthy to nurse in my minde,
Thirst to come backe; oh if thou die before,
My soule from other lands to thee shall soare.
Thy (else Almighty) beautie cannot move
Rage from the Seas, nor thy love teach them love,
Nor tame wilde Boreas harshnesse; Thou hast reade
How roughly hee in peeces shivered
Faire Orithea, whom he swore he lov'd.
Fall ill or good, 'tis madnesse to have prov'd
Dangers unurg'd; Feed on this flattery,
That absent Lovers one in th'other be.
Dissemble nothing, not a boy, nor change
Thy bodies habite, nor mindes; bee not strange
To thy selfe onely; All will spie in thy face
A blushing womanly discovering grace;
Richly cloath'd Apes, are call'd Apes, and as soone
Ecclips'd as bright we call the Moone the Moone.
Men of France, changeable Camelions,
Spittles of diseases, shops of fashions,
Loves fuellers, and the rightest company
Of Players, which upon the worlds stage be,
Will quickly know thee, and no lesse, alas!
Th'indifferent Italian, as we passe
His warme land, well content to thinke thee Page,
Will hunt thee with such lust, and hideous rage,
As Lots faire guests were vext. But none of these
Nor spungy hydroptique Dutch shall thee displease,
If thou stay here. O stay here, for, for thee,
England is onely a worthy Gallerie,
To walke in expectation, till from thence
Our greatest King call thee to his presence.
When I am gone, dreame me some happinesse,
Nor let thy lookes our long hid love confesse,
Nor praise, nor dispraise me, nor blesse nor curse

Openly loves force, nor in bed fright thy Nurse
With midnights startings, crying out, oh, oh
Nurse, oh my love is slaine, I saw him goe
O'r the white Alpes alone; I saw him I,
Assail'd, fight, taken, stabb'd, bleed, fall, and die.
Augure me better chance, except dread Jove
Thinke it enough for me to'have had thy love.

To his Mistris Going to Bed

Come, Madam, come, all rest my powers defie,
Until I labour, I in labour lie.
The foe oft-times having the foe in sight,
Is tir'd with standing though he never fight.
Off with that girdle, like heavens Zone glittering,
But a far fairer world incompassing.
Unpin that spangled breastplate which you wear,
That th'eyes of busie fooles may be stopt there.
Unlace your self, for that harmonious chyme,
Tells me from you, that now it is bed time.
Off with that happy busk, which I envie,
That still can be, and still can stand so nigh.
Your gown going off, such beautious state reveals,
As when from flowry meads th'hills shadow steales.
Off with that wyerie Coronet and shew
The haiery Diademe which on you doth grow:
Now off with those shooes, and then safely tread
In this loves hallow'd temple, this soft bed.
In such white robes, heaven's Angels us'd to be
Receavd by men; Thou Angel bringst with thee
A heaven like Mahomets Paradise; and though
Ill spirits walk in white, we easly know,
By this these Angels from an evil sprite,
Those set our hairs, but these our flesh upright.
        Licence my roaving hands, and let them go,
Before, behind, between, above, below.
O my America! my new-found-land,
My kingdome, safeliest when with one man man'd,
My Myne of precious stones, My Emperie,

How blest am I in this discovering thee!
To enter in these bonds, is to be free;
Then where my hand is set, my seal shall be.
　　　Full nakedness! All joyes are due to thee,
As souls unbodied, bodies uncloth'd must be,
To taste whole joyes. Gems which you women use
Are like Atlanta's balls, cast in mens views,
That when a fools eye lighteth on a Gem,
His earthly soul may covet theirs, not them.
Like pictures, or like books gay coverings made
For lay-men, are all women thus array'd;
Themselves are mystick books, which only wee
(Whom their imputed grace will dignifie)
Must see reveal'd. Then since that I may know;
As liberally, as to a Midwife, shew
Thy self: cast all, yea, this white lynnen hence,
There is no pennance due to innocence.
　　　To teach thee, I am naked first; why than
What needst thou have more covering then a man.

The Calme

Our storme is past, and that storms tyrannous rage,
A stupid calme, but nothing it, doth swage.
The fable is inverted, and farre more
A blocke afflicts, now, then a storke before.
Stormes chafe, and soone weare out themselves, or us;
In calmes, Heaven laughs to see us languish thus.
As steady'as I can wish, that my thoughts were,
Smooth as thy mistresse glasse, or what shines there,
The sea is now. And, as the Iles which wee
Seeke, when wee can move, our ships rooted bee.
As water did in stormes, now pitch runs out:
As lead, when a fir'd Church becomes one spout.
And all our beauty, and our trimme, decayes,
Like courts removing, or like ended playes.
The fighting place now seamens ragges supply;
And all the tackling is a frippery.
No use of lanthornes; and in one place lay

Feathers and dust, to day and yesterday.
Earths hollownesses, which the worlds lungs are,
Have no more winde then the upper valt of aire.
We can nor lost friends, nor sought foes recover,
But meteorlike, save that wee move not, hover.
Onely the Calenture together drawes
Deare friends, which meet dead in great fishes jawes:
And on the hatches as on Altars lyes
Each one, his owne Priest, and owne Sacrifice.
Who live, that miracle do multiply
Where walkers in hot Ovens, doe not dye.
If in despite of these, wee swimme, that hath
No more refreshing, then our brimstone Bath,
But from the sea, into the ship we turne,
Like parboyl'd wretches, on the coales to burne.
Like *Bajazet* encag'd, the shepheards scoffe,
Or like slacke sinew'd *Sampson,* his haire off,
Languish our ships. Now, as a Miriade
Of Ants, durst th'Emperours lov'd snake invade,
The crawling Gallies, Sea-goales, finny chips,
Might brave our Pinnaces, now bed-ridde ships.
Whether a rotten state, and hope of gaine,
Or to disuse mee from the queasie paine
Of being belov'd, and loving, or the thirst
Of honour, or faire death, out pusht mee first,
I lose my end: for here as well as I
A desperate may live, and a coward die.
Stagge, dogge, and all which from, or towards flies,
Is paid with life, or pray, or doing dyes.
Fate grudges us all, and doth subtly lay
A scourge,'gainst which wee all forget to pray,
He that at sea prayes for more winde, as well
Under the poles may begge cold, heat in hell.
What are wee then? How little more alas
Is man now, then before he was? he was
Nothing; for us, wee are for nothing fit;
Chance, or our selves still disproportion it.
Wee have no power, no will, no sense; I lye,
I should not then thus feele this miserie.

The Flea

Marke but this flea, and marke in this,
How little that which thou deny'st me is;
It suck'd me first, and now sucks thee,
And in this flea, our two bloods mingled bee;
Thou know'st that this cannot be said
A sinne, nor shame, nor losse of maidenhead,
    Yet this enjoyes before it wooe,
      And pamper'd swells with one blood made of two,
      And this, alas, is more then wee would doe.

Oh stay, three lives in one flea spare,
Where wee almost, yea more then maryed are,
This flea is you and I, and this
Our mariage bed, and mariage temple is;
Though parents grudge, and you, w'are met,
And cloysterd in these living walls of Jet.
    Though use make you apt to kill mee,
      Let not to that, selfe murder added bee,
      And sacrilege, three sinnes in killing three.

Cruell and sodaine, hast thou since
Purpled thy naile, in blood of innocence?
Wherein could this flea guilty bee,
Except in that drop which it suckt from thee?
Yet thou triumph'st, and saist that thou
Find'st not thy selfe, nor mee the weaker now;
    'Tis true, then learne how false, feares bee;
      Just so much honor, when thou yeeld'st to mee,
      Will wast, as this flea's death tooke life from thee.

The Good-Morrow

I wonder by my troth, what thou, and I
Did, till we lov'd? were we not wean'd till then?
But suck'd on countrey pleasures, childishly?
Or snorted we in the seaven sleepers den?
T'was so; But this, all pleasures fancies bee.
If ever any beauty I did see,
Which I desir'd, and got, t'was but a dreame of thee.

And now good morrow to our waking soules,
Which watch not one another out of feare;
For love, all love of other sights controules,
And makes one little roome, an every where.
Let sea-discoverers to new worlds have gone,
Let Maps to other, worlds on worlds have showne,
Let us possesse one world, each hath one, and is one.

My face in thine eye, thine in mine appeares,
And true plain hearts doe in the faces rest,
Where can we finde two better hemispheares
Without sharpe North, without declining West?
What ever dyes, was not mixt equally;
If our two loves be one, or, thou and I
Love so alike, that none doe slacken, none can die.

Song

Goe, and catche a falling starre,
   Get with child a mandrake roote,
Tell me where all past yeares are,
   Or who cleft the Divels foot,
Teach me to heare Mermaides singing,
   Or to keep off envies stinging,
        And finde
        What winde
Serves to advance an honest minde.

If thou beest borne to strange sights,
   Things invisible to see,
Ride ten thousand daies and nights,
   Till age snow white haires on thee,
Thou, when thou retorn'st, wilt tell mee
All strange wonders that befell thee,
        And sweare
        No where
Lives a woman true, and faire.

If thou findst one, let mee know,
   Such a Pilgrimage were sweet;
Yet doe not, I would not goe,
   Though at next doore wee might meet,
Though shee were true, when you met her,
And last, till you write your letter,
        Yet shee
        Will bee
False, ere I come, to two, or three.

The Sunne Rising

        Busie old foole, unruly Sunne,
        Why dost thou thus,
Through windowes, and through curtaines call on us?
Must to thy motions lovers seasons run?
        Sawcy pedantique wretch, goe chide
        Late schoole boyes, and sowre prentices,
    Goe tell Court-huntsmen, that the King will ride,
    Call countrey ants to harvest offices;
Love, all alike, no season knowes, nor clyme,
Nor houres, dayes, moneths, which are the rags of time.

        Thy beames, so reverend, and strong
        Why shouldst thou thinke?
I could eclipse and cloud them with a winke,
But that I would not lose her sight so long:
        If her eyes have not blinded thine,
        Looke, and to morrow late, tell mee,
    Whether both the'India's of spice and Myne
    Be where thou leftst them, or lie here with mee.
Aske for those Kings whom thou saw'st yesterday,
And thou shalt heare, All here in one bed lay.

        She'is all States, and all Princes, I,
        Nothing else is.
Princes doe but play us; compar'd to this,
All honor's mimique; All wealth alchimie.
        Thou sunne art halfe as happy'as wee,
        In that the world's contracted thus;
    Thine age askes ease, and since thy duties bee
    To warme the world, that's done in warming us.
Shine here to us, and thou art every where;
This bed thy center is, these walls, thy spheare.

The Canonization

For Godsake hold your tongue, and let me love,
  Or chide my palsie, or my gout,
My five gray haires, or ruin'd fortune flout,
    With wealth your state, your minde with Arts improve,
      Take you a course, get you a place,
      Observe his honour, or his grace,
Or the Kings reall, or his stamped face
    Contemplate, what you will, approve,
    So you will let me love.

Alas, alas, who's injur'd by my love?
  What merchants ships have my sighs drown'd?
Who saies my teares have overflow'd his ground?
    When did my colds a forward spring remove?
      When did the heats which my veines fill
      Adde one more to the plaguie Bill?
Soldiers finde warres, and Lawyers finde out still
    Litigious men, which quarrels move,
    Though she and I do love.

Call us what you will, wee are made such by love;
  Call her one, mee another flye,
We'are Tapers too, and at our owne cost die,
    And wee in us finde the'Eagle and the Dove.
      The Phœnix ridle hath more wit
      By us, we two being one, are it.
So, to one neutrall thing both sexes fit,
    Wee dye and rise the same, and prove
    Mysterious by this love.

Wee can dye by it, if not live by love,
  And if unfit for tombes and hearse
Our legend bee, it will be fit for verse;
    And if no peece of Chronicle wee prove,
      We'll build in sonnets pretty roomes;
      As well a well wrought urne becomes
The greatest ashes, as halfe-acre tombes,
    And by these hymns, all shall approve
    Us *Canoniz'd* for Love:

And thus invoke us; You whom reverend love
   Made one anothers hermitage;
You, to whom love was peace, that now is rage;
    Who did the whole worlds soule contract, and drove
     Into the glasses of your eyes
      So made such mirrors, and such spies,
That they did all to you epitomize,
    Countries, Townes, Courts: Beg from above
    A patterne of your love!

Song

    Sweetest love, I do not goe,
     For wearinesse of thee,
    Nor in hope the world can show
     A fitter Love for mee;
      But since that I
    Must dye at last, 'tis best,
    To use my selfe in jest
     Thus by fain'd deaths to dye;

    Yesternight the Sunne went hence,
     And yet is here to day,
    He hath no desire nor sense,
     Nor halfe so short a way:
      Then feare not mee,
    But beleeve that I shall make
    Speedier journeyes, since I take
     More wings and spurres then hee.

    O how feeble is mans power,
     That if good fortune fall,
    Cannot adde another houre,
     Nor a lost houre recall!
      But come bad chance,
    And wee joyne to'it our strength,
    And wee teach it art and length,
     It selfe o'r us to'advance.

When thou sigh'st, thou sigh'st not winde,
  But sigh'st my soule away,
When thou weep'st, unkindly kinde,
  My lifes blood doth decay.
    It cannot bee
That thou lov'st mee, as thou say'st,
If in thine my life thou waste,
  Thou art the best of mee.

Let not thy divining heart
  Forethinke me any ill,
Destiny may take thy part,
  And may thy feares fulfill;
    But thinke that wee
Are but turn'd aside to sleepe;
They who one another keepe
  Alive, ne'r parted bee.

Aire and Angells

Twice or thrice had I loved thee,
Before I knew thy face or name,
So in a voice, so in a shapelesse flame,
Angells affect us oft, and worship'd bee;
  Still when, to where thou wert, I came,
Some lovely glorious nothing I did see.
  But since my soule, whose child love is,
Takes limmes of flesh, and else could nothing doe,
  More subtile then the parent is,
Love must not be, but take a body too,
  And therefore what thou wert, and who,
    I bid Love aske, and now
That it assume thy body, I allow,
And fixe it selfe in thy lip, eye, and brow.

Whilst thus to ballast love, I thought,
And so more steddily to have gone,
With wares which would sinke admiration,
I saw, I had loves pinnace overfraught,
   Ev'ry thy haire for love to worke upon
Is much too much, some fitter must be sought;
   For, nor in nothing, nor in things
Extreme, and scatt'ring bright, can love inhere;
   Then as an Angell, face, and wings
Of aire, not pure as it, yet pure doth weare,
   So thy love may be my loves spheare;
      Just such disparitie
As is twixt Aire and Angells puritie,
'Twixt womens love, and mens will ever bee.

The Anniversarie

All Kings, and all their favorites,
   All glory of honors, beauties, wits,
The Sun it selfe, which makes times, as they passe,
Is elder by a yeare, now, then it was
When thou and I first one another saw:
All other things, to their destruction draw,
   Only our love hath no decay;
This, no to morrow hath, nor yesterday,
Running it never runs from us away,
But truly keepes his first, last, everlasting day.

Two graves must hide thine and my coarse,
   If one might, death were no divorce,
Alas, as well as other Princes, wee,
(Who Prince enough in one another bee,)
Must leave at last in death, these eyes, and eares,
Oft fed with true oathes, and with sweet salt teares;
   But soules where nothing dwells but love
(All other thoughts being inmates) then shall prove
This, or a love increased there above,
When bodies to their graves, soules from their graves
   remove.

And then wee shall be throughly blest,
  But wee no more, then all the rest;
Here upon earth, we'are Kings, and none but wee
Can be such Kings, nor of such subjects bee;
Who is so safe as wee? where none can doe
Treason to us, except one of us two.
  True and false feares let us refraine,
Let us love nobly, and live, and adde againe
Yeares and yeares unto yeares, till we attaine
To write threescore: this is the second of our raigne.

Loves Growth

I scarce beleeve my love to be so pure
  As I had thought it was,
  Because it doth endure
Vicissitude, and season, as the grasse;
Me thinkes I lyed all winter, when I swore,
My love was infinite, if spring make'it more.

But if this medicine, love, which cures all sorrow
With more, not onely bee no quintessence,
But mixt of all stuffes, paining soule, or sense,
And of the Sunne his working vigour borrow,
Love's not so pure, and abstract, as they use
To say, which have no Mistresse but their Muse,
But as all else, being elemented too,
Love sometimes would contemplate, sometimes do.

And yet no greater, but more eminent,
  Love by the spring is growne;
  As, in the firmament,
Starres by the Sunne are not inlarg'd, but showne.
Gentle love deeds, as blossomes on a bough,
From loves awakened root do bud out now.

If, as in water stir'd more circles bee
Produc'd by one, love such additions take,
Those like so many spheares, but one heaven make,
For, they are all concentrique unto thee;

And though each spring doe adde to love new heate,
As princes doe in times of action get
New taxes, and remit them not in peace,
No winter shall abate the springs encrease.

The Dreame

Deare love, for nothing lesse then thee
Would I have broke this happy dreame,
     It was a theame
For reason, much too strong for phantasie,
Therefore thou wakd'st me wisely; yet
My Dreame thou brok'st not, but continued'st it,
Thou art so truth, that thoughts of thee suffice,
To make dreames truths; and fables histories;
Enter these armes, for since thou thoughtst it best,
Not to dreame all my dreame, let's act the rest.

As lightning, or a Tapers light,
Thine eyes, and not thy noise wak'd mee;
     Yet I thought thee
(For thou lovest truth) an Angell, at first sight,
But when I saw thou sawest my heart,
And knew'st my thoughts, beyond an Angells art,
When thou knew'st what I dreamt, when thou knew'st when
Excesse of joy would wake me, and cam'st then,
I must confesse, it could not chuse but bee
Prophane, to thinke thee any thing but thee.

Comming and staying show'd thee, thee,
But rising makes me doubt, that now,
     Thou art not thou.
That love is weake, where feare's as strong as hee;
'Tis not all spirit, pure, and brave,
If mixture it of *Feare, Shame, Honor,* have.
Perchance as torches which must ready bee,
Men light and put out, so thou deal'st with mee,
Thou cam'st to kindle, goest to come; Then I
Will dreame that hope againe, but else would die.

A Valediction: Of Weeping

Let me powre forth
My teares before thy face, whil'st I stay here,
For thy face coines them, and thy stampe they beare,
And by this Mintage they are something worth,
For thus they bee
Pregnant of thee;
Fruits of much griefe they are, emblemes of more,
When a teare falls, that thou falst which it bore,
So thou and I are nothing then, when on a divers shore.

On a round ball
A workeman that hath copies by, can lay
An Europe, Afrique, and an Asia,
And quickly make that, which was nothing, *All*,
So doth each teare,
Which thee doth weare,
A globe, yea world by that impression grow,
Till thy teares mixt with mine doe overflow
This world, by waters sent from thee, my heaven dissolved so.

O more then Moone,
Draw not up seas to drowne me in thy spheare,
Weepe me not dead, in thine armes, but forbeare
To teach the sea, what it may doe too soone;
Let not the winde
Example finde,
To doe me more harme, then it purposeth;
Since thou and I sigh one anothers breath,
Who e'r sighes most, is cruellest, and hasts the others death.

Loves Alchymie

Some that have deeper digg'd loves Myne then I,
Say, where his centrique happinesse doth lie:
      I have lov'd, and got, and told,
But should I love, get, tell, till I were old,
I should not finde that hidden mysterie;
      Oh, 'tis imposture all:
And as no chymique yet th'Elixar got,
      But glorifies his pregnant pot,
      If by the way to him befall
Some odoriferous thing, or medicinall,
 So, lovers dreame a rich and long delight,
 But get a winter-seeming summers night.

Our ease, our thrift, our honor, and our day,
Shall we, for this vaine Bubles shadow pay?
      Ends love in this, that my man,
Can be as happy'as I can; If he can
Endure the short scorne of a Bridegroomes play?
      That loving wretch that sweares,
'Tis not the bodies marry, but the mindes,
      Which he in her Angelique findes,
      Would sweare as justly, that he heares,
In that dayes rude hoarse minstralsey, the spheares.
 Hope not for minde in women; at their best
 Sweetnesse and wit, they'are but *Mummy*, possest.

A Nocturnall upon S. Lucies Day,
being the shortest day

'Tis the yeares midnight, and it is the dayes,
Lucies, who scarce seaven houres herself unmaskes,
   The Sunne is spent, and now his flasks
   Send forth light squibs, no constant rayes;
      The worlds whole sap is sunke:
The generall balme th'hydroptique earth hath drunk,
Whither, as to the beds-feet, life is shrunke,
Dead and enterr'd; yet all these seeme to laugh,
Compar'd with mee, who am their Epitaph.

Study me then, you who shall lovers bee
At the next world, that is, at the next Spring:
   For I am every dead thing,
   In whom love wrought new Alchimie.
      For his art did expresse
A quintessence even from nothingnesse,
From dull privations, and leane emptinesse:
He ruin'd mee, and I am re-begot
Of absence, darknesse, death; things which are not.

All others, from all things, draw all that's good,
Life, soule, forme, spirit, whence they beeing have;
   I, by loves limbecke, am the grave
   Of all, that's nothing. Oft a flood
      Have wee two wept, and so
Drownd the whole world, us two; oft did we grow
To be two Chaosses, when we did show
Care to ought else; and often absences
Withdrew our soules, and made us carcasses.

But I am by her death, (which word wrongs her)
Of the first nothing, the Elixer grown;
   Were I a man, that I were one,
   I needs must know; I should preferre,
      If I were any beast,

Some ends, some means; Yea plants, yea stones detest,
And love; All, all some properties invest;
If I an ordinary nothing were,
As shadow, a light, and body must be here.

But I am None; nor will my Sunne renew.
You lovers, for whose sake, the lesser Sunne
    At this time to the Goat is runne
    To fetch new lust, and give it you,
        Enjoy your summer all;
Since shee enjoyes her long nights festivall,
Let mee prepare towards her, and let mee call
This houre her Vigill, and her Eve, since this
Both the yeares, and the dayes deep midnight is.

The Apparition

When by thy scorne, O murdresse, I am dead,
And that thou thinkst thee free
From all solicitation from mee,
Then shall my ghost come to thy bed,
And thee, fain'd vestall, in worse armes shall see;
Then thy sicke taper will begin to winke,
And he, whose thou art then, being tyr'd before,
Will, if thou stirre, or pinch to wake him, thinke
        Thou call'st for more,
And in false sleepe will from thee shrinke,
And then poore Aspen wretch, neglected thou
Bath'd in a cold quicksilver sweat wilt lye
        A veryer ghost then I;
What I will say, I will not tell thee now,
Lest that preserve thee'; and since my love is spent,
I'had rather thou shouldst painfully repent,
Then by my threatnings rest still innocent.

A Valediction: Forbidding Mourning

As virtuous men passe mildly away,
   And whisper to their soules, to goe,
Whilst some of their sad friends doe say,
   The breath goes now, and some say, no:

So let us melt, and make no noise,
   No teare-floods, nor sigh-tempests move,
T'were prophanation of our joyes
   To tell the layetie our love.

Moving of th'earth brings harmes and feares,
   Men reckon what it did and meant,
But trepidation of the spheares,
   Though greater farre, is innocent.

Dull sublunary lovers love
   (Whose soule is sense) cannot admit
Absence, because it doth remove
   Those things which elemented it.

But we by a love, so much refin'd,
   That our selves know not what it is,
Inter-assured of the mind,
   Care lesse, eyes, lips, and hands to misse.

Our two soules therefore, which are one,
   Though I must goe, endure not yet
A breach, but an expansion,
   Like gold to ayery thinnesse beate.

If they be two, they are two so
   As stiffe twin compasses are two,
Thy soule the fixt foot, makes no show
   To move, but doth, if the'other doe.

And though it in the center sit,
    Yet when the other far doth rome,
It leanes, and hearkens after it,
    And growes erect, as that comes home.

Such wilt thou be to mee, who must
    Like th'other foot, obliquely runne;
Thy firmnes makes my circle just,
    And makes me end, where I begunne.

The Extasie

Where, like a pillow on a bed,
    A Pregnant banke swel'd up, to rest
The violets reclining head,
    Sat we two, one anothers best.
Our hands were firmely cimented
    With a fast balme, which thence did spring,
Our eye-beames twisted, and did thred
    Our eyes, upon one double string;
So to'entergraft our hands, as yet
    Was all the meanes to make us one,
And pictures in our eyes to get
    Was all our propagation.
As 'twixt two equal Armies, Fate
    Suspends uncertaine victorie,
Our soules, (which to advance their state,
    Were gone out,) hung 'twixt her, and mee.
And whil'st our soules negotiate there,
    Wee like sepulchrall statues lay;
All day, the same our postures were,
    And wee said nothing, all the day.
If any, so by love refin'd,
    That he soules language understood,
And by good love were growen all minde,
    Within convenient distance stood,
He (though he knew not which soule spake,
    Because both meant, both spake the same)

Might thence a new concoction take,
    And part farre purer then he came.
This Extasie doth unperplex
    (We said) and tell us what we love,
Wee see by this, it was not sexe,
    Wee see, we saw not what did move:
But as all severall soules containe
    Mixture of things, they know not what,
Love, these mixt soules doth mixe againe,
    And makes both one, each this and that.
A single violet transplant,
    The strength, the colour, and the size,
(All which before was poore, and scant,)
    Redoubles still, and multiplies.
When love, with one another so
    Interinanimates two soules,
That abler soule, which thence doth flow,
    Defects of lonelinesse controules.
Wee then, who are this new soule, know,
    Of what we are compos'd, and made,
For, th'Atomies of which we grow,
    Are soules, whom no change can invade.
But O alas, so long, so farre
    Our bodies why doe wee forbeare?
They'are ours, though they'are not wee, Wee are
    The intelligences, they the spheare.
We owe them thankes, because they thus,
    Did us, to us, at first convay,
Yeelded their forces, sense, to us,
    Nor are drosse to us, but allay.
On man heavens influence workes not so,
    But that it first imprints the ayre,
Soe soule into the soule may flow,
    Though it to body first repaire.
As our blood labours to beget
    Spirits, as like soules as it can,
Because such fingers need to knit
    That subtile knot, which makes us man:
So must pure lovers soules descend
    T'affections, and to faculties,

Which sense may reach and apprehend,
  Else a great Prince in prison lies.
To'our bodies turne wee then, that so
  Weake men on love reveal'd may looke;
Loves mysteries in soules doe grow,
  But yet the body is his booke.
And if some lover, such as wee,
  Have heard this dialogue of one,
Let him still marke us, he shall see
  Small change, when we'are to bodies gone.

Loves Deitie

I long to talke with some old lovers ghost,
  Who dyed before the god of Love was borne:
I cannot thinke that hee, who then lov'd most,
  Sunke so low, as to love one which did scorne.
But since this god produc'd a destinie,
And that vice-nature, custome, lets it be;
  I must love her, that loves not mee.

Sure, they which made him god, meant not so much,
  Nor he, in his young godhead practis'd it;
But when an even flame two hearts did touch,
  His office was indulgently to fit
Actives to passives. Correspondencie
Only his subject was; It cannot bee
  Love, till I love her, that loves mee.

But every moderne god will now extend
  His vast prerogative, as far as Jove.
To rage, to lust, to write to, to commend,
  All is the purlewe of the God of Love.
Oh were wee wak'ned by this Tyrannie
To ungod this child againe, it could not bee
  I should love her, who loves not mee.

Rebell and Atheist too, why murmure I,
   As though I felt the worst that love could doe?
Love might make me leave loving, or might trie
   A deeper plague, to make her love me too,
Which, since she loves before, I'am loth to see;
Falshood is worse then hate; and that must bee,
   If shee whom I love, should love mee.

The Will

Before I sigh my last gaspe, let me breath,
   Great love, some Legacies; Here I bequeath
Mine eyes to Argus, if mine eyes can see,
If they be blinde, then Love, I give them thee;
My tongue to Fame; to'Embassadours mine eares;
   To women or the sea, my teares.
   Thou, Love, hast taught mee heretofore
By making mee serve her who'had twenty more,
That I should give to none, but such, as had too much
   before.

My constancie I to the planets give;
My truth to them, who at the Court doe live;
Mine ingenuity and opennesse,
To Jesuites; to Buffones my pensivenesse;
My silence to'any, who abroad hath beene;
   My mony to a Capuchin.
   Thou Love taught'st me, by appointing mee
To love there, where no love receiv'd can be,
Onely to give to such as have an incapacitie.

My faith I give to Roman Catholiques;
All my good works unto the Schismaticks
Of Amsterdam; my best civility
And Courtship, to an Universitie;
My modesty I give to souldiers bare;
   My patience let gamesters share.
   Thou Love taughtst mee, by making mee
Love her that holds my love disparity,
Onely to give to those that count my gifts indignity.

I give my reputation to those
Which were my friends; Mine industrie to foes;
To Schoolemen I bequeath my doubtfulnesse;
My sicknesse to Physitians, or excesse;
To Nature, all that I in Ryme have writ;
   And to my company my wit.
  Thou Love, by making mee adore
Her, who begot this love in mee before,
Taughtst me to make, as though I gave, when I did but
    restore.

To him for whom the passing bell next tolls,
I give my physick bookes; my writen rowles
Of Morall counsels, I to Bedlam give;
My brazen medals, unto them which live
In want of bread; To them which passe among
    All forrainers, mine English tongue.
   Thou, Love, by making mee love one
Who thinkes her friendship a fit portion
For yonger lovers, dost my gifts thus disproportion.

Therefore I'll give no more; But I'll undoe
The world by dying; because love dies too.
Then all your beauties will bee no more worth
Then gold in Mines, where none doth draw it forth;
And all your graces no more use shall have
    Then a Sun dyall in a grave.
   Thou Love taughtst mee, by making mee
Love her, who doth neglect both mee and thee,
To'invent, and practise this one way, to'annihilate all three.

The Expiration

So, so, breake off this last lamenting kisse,
    Which sucks two soules, and vapors Both away,
Turne thou ghost that way, and let mee turne this,
    And let our selves benight our happiest day,
We ask'd none leave to love; nor will we owe
    Any, so cheape a death, as saying, Goe;

Goe; and if that word have not quite kil'd thee,
    Ease mee with death, by bidding mee goe too.
Or, if it have, let my word worke on mee,
    And a just office on a murderer doe.
Except it be too late, to kill me so,
    Being double dead, going, and bidding, goe.

The Funerall

Who ever comes to shroud me, do not harme
        Nor question much
That subtile wreath of haire, which crowns my arme;
The mystery, the signe you must not touch,
        For 'tis my outward Soule,
Viceroy to that, which then to heaven being gone,
        Will leave this to controule,
And keepe these limbes, her Provinces, from dissolution.

For if the sinewie thread my braine lets fall
        Through every part,
Can tye those parts, and make mee one of all;
These haires which upward grew, and strength and art
        Have from a better braine,
Can better do'it; Except she meant that I
        By this should know my pain,
As prisoners then are manacled, when they'are condemn'd to
    die.

What ere shee meant by'it, bury it with me,
    For since I am
Loves martyr, it might breed idolatrie,
If into others hands these Reliques came;
    As 'twas humility
To afford to it all that a Soule can doe,
    So,'tis some bravery,
That since you would save none of mee, I bury some of you.

Holy Sonnet I

Thou hast made me, And shall thy worke decay?
Repaire me now, for now mine end doth haste,
I runne to death, and death meets me as fast,
And all my pleasures are like yesterday;
I dare not move my dimme eyes any way,
Despaire behind, and death before doth cast
Such terrour, and my feeble flesh doth waste
By sinne in it, which it t'wards hell doth weigh;
Onely thou art above, and when towards thee
By thy leave I can looke, I rise againe;
But our old subtle foe so tempteth me,
That not one houre my selfe I can sustaine;
Thy Grace may wing me to prevent his art,
And thou like Adamant draw mine iron heart.

Holy Sonnet II

As due by many titles I resigne
My selfe to thee, O God, first I was made
By thee, and for thee, and when I was decay'd
Thy blood bought that, the which before was thine;
I am thy sonne, made with thy selfe to shine,
Thy servant, whose paines thou hast still repaid,
Thy sheepe, thine Image, and, till I betray'd
My selfe, a temple of thy Spirit divine;
Why doth the devill then usurpe on mee?
Why doth he steale, nay ravish that's thy right?
Except thou rise and for thine owne worke fight,
Oh I shall soone despaire, when I doe see
That thou lov'st mankind well, yet wilt'not chuse me.
And Satan hates mee, yet is loth to lose mee.

Holy Sonnet IV

Oh my blacke Soule! now thou art summoned
By sicknesse, deaths herald, and champion;
Thou art like a pilgrim, which abroad hath done
Treason, and durst not turne to whence hee is fled,
Or like a thiefe, which till deaths doome be read,
Wisheth himselfe delivered from prison;
But damn'd and hal'd to execution,
Wisheth that still he might be imprisoned.
Yet grace, if thou repent, thou canst not lacke;
But who shall give thee that grace to beginne?
Oh make thy selfe with holy mourning blacke,
And red with blushing, as thou art with sinne;
Or wash thee in Christs blood, which hath this might
That being red, it dyes red soules to white.

Holy Sonnet VII

At the round earths imagin'd corners, blow
Your trumpets, Angells, and arise, arise
From death, you numberlesse infinities
Of soules, and to your scattred bodies goe,
All whom the flood did, and fire shall o'erthrow,
All whom warre, dearth, age, agues, tyrannies,
Despaire, law, chance, hath slaine, and you whose eyes,
Shall behold God, and never tast deaths woe.
But let them sleepe, Lord, and mee mourne a space,
For, if above all these, my sinnes abound,
'Tis late to aske abundance of thy grace,
When wee are there; here on this lowly ground,
Teach mee how to repent; for that's as good
As if thou'hadst seal'd my pardon, with thy blood.

Holy Sonnet IX

If poysonous mineralls, and if that tree,
Whose fruit threw death on else immortall us,
If lecherous goats, if serpents envious
Cannot be damn'd; Alas; why should I bee?
Why should intent or reason, borne in mee,
Make sinnes, else equall, in mee more heinous?
And mercy being easie, and glorious
To God; in his sterne wrath, why threatens hee?
But who am I, that dare dispute with thee
O God? Oh! of thine onely worthy blood,
And my teares, make a heavenly Lethean flood,
And drowne in it my sinnes blacke memorie;
That thou remember them, some claime as debt,
I thinke it mercy, if thou wilt forget.

Holy Sonnet X

Death be not proud, though some have called thee
Mighty and dreadfull, for, thou art not soe,
For, those, whom thou think'st, thou dost overthrow,
Die not, poore death, nor yet canst thou kill mee.
From rest and sleepe, which but thy pictures bee,
Much pleasure, then from thee, much more must flow,
And soonest our best men with thee doe goe,
Rest of their bones, and soules deliverie.
Thou art slave to Fate, Chance, kings, and desperate men,
And dost with poyson, warre, and sicknesse dwell,
And poppie, or charmes can make us sleepe as well,
And better then thy stroake; why swell'st thou then?
One short sleepe past, wee wake eternally,
And death shall be no more; death, thou shalt die.

Holy Sonnet XI

Spit in my face you Jewes, and pierce my side,
Buffet, and scoffe, scourge and crucifie mee,
For I have sinn'd, and sinn'd, and onely hee,
Who could do no iniquitie, hath dyed:
But by my death can not be satisfied
My sinnes, which passe the Jewes impiety:
They kill'd once an inglorious man, but I
Crucifie him daily, being now glorified.
Oh let mee then, his strange love still admire:
Kings pardon, but he bore our punishment.
And *Jacob* came cloth'd in vile harsh attire
But to supplant, and with gainfull intent:
God cloth'd himselfe in vile mans flesh, that so
Hee might be weake enough to suffer woe.

Holy Sonnet XIV

Batter my heart, three person'd God; for, you
As yet but knocke, breathe, shine, and seeke to mend;
That I may rise, and stand, o'erthrow mee,'and bend
Your force, to breake, blowe, burn and make me new.
I, like an usurpt towne, to'another due,
Labour to'admit you, but Oh, to no end,
Reason your viceroy in mee, mee should defend,
But is captiv'd, and proves weake or untrue.
Yet dearely'I love you,'and would be loved faine,
But am betroth'd unto your enemie:
Divorce mee,'untie, or breake that knot againe,
Take mee to you, imprison mee, for I
Except you'enthrall mee, never shall be free,
Nor ever chast, except you ravish mee.

Holy Sonnet XVII

Since she whom I lov'd hath payd her last debt
To Nature, and to hers, and my good is dead,
And her Soule early into heaven ravished,
Wholly on heavenly things my mind is sett.
Here the admyring her my mind did whett
To seeke thee God; so streames do shew their head;
But though I have found thee, and thou my thirst hast fed,
A holy thirsty dropsy melts mee yett.
But why should I begg more Love, when as thou
Dost wooe my soule for hers; offring all thine:
And dost not only feare least I allow
My Love to Saints and Angels, things divine,
But in thy tender jealosy dost doubt
Least the World, Fleshe, yea Devill putt thee out.

Good Friday, 1613.
Riding Westward

Let mans Soule be a Spheare, and then, in this,
The intelligence that moves, devotion is,
And as the other Spheares, by being growne
Subject to forraigne motions, lose their owne,
And being by others hurried every day,
Scarce in a yeare their naturall forme obey:
Pleasure or businesse, so, our Soules admit
For their first mover, and are whirld by it.
Hence is't, that I am carryed towards the West
This day, when my Soules forme bends toward the East.
There I should see a Sunne, by rising set,
And by that setting endlesse day beget;
But that Christ on this Crosse, did rise and fall,
Sinne had eternally benighted all.
Yet dare I'almost be glad, I do not see
That spectacle of too much weight for mee.
Who sees Gods face, that is selfe life, must dye;
What a death were it then to see God dye?
It made his owne Lieutenant Nature shrinke,
It made his footstoole crack, and the Sunne winke.
Could I behold those hands which span the Poles,
And turne all spheares at once, peirc'd with those holes?
Could I behold that endlesse height which is
Zenith to us, and our Antipodes,
Humbled below us? or that blood which is
The seat of all our Soules, if not of his,
Made durt of dust, or that flesh which was worne
By God, for his apparell, rag'd, and torne?
If on these things I durst not looke, durst I
Upon his miserable mother cast mine eye,
Who was Gods partner here, and furnish'd thus
Halfe of that Sacrifice, which ransom'd us?
Though these things, as I ride, be from mine eye,
They'are present yet unto my memory,
For that looks towards them; and thou look'st towards mee,

O Saviour, as thou hang'st upon the tree;
I turne my backe to thee, but to receive
Corrections, till thy mercies bid thee leave.
O thinke mee worth thine anger, punish mee,
Burne off my rusts, and my deformity,
Restore thine Image, so much, by thy grace,
That thou may'st know mee, and I'll turne my face.

A Hymne to Christ, at the Authors last going into Germany

In what torne ship soever I embarke,
That ship shall be my embleme of thy Arke;
What sea soever swallow mee, that flood
Shall be to mee an embleme of thy blood;
Though thou with clouds of anger do disguise
Thy face; yet through that maske I know those eyes,
    Which; though they turne away sometimes,
        They never will despise.

I sacrifice this Iland unto thee,
And all whom I lov'd there, and who lov'd mee;
When I have put our seas twixt them and mee,
Put thou thy sea betwixt my sinnes and thee.
As the trees sap doth seeke the root below
In winter, in my winter now I goe,
    Where none but thee, th'Eternall root
        Of true Love I may know.

Nor thou nor thy religion dost controule,
The amorousnesse of an harmonious Soule,
But thou would'st have that love thy selfe: As thou
Art jealous, Lord, so I am jealous now,
Thou lov'st not, till from loving more, thou free
My soule: Who ever gives, takes libertie:
    O, if thou car'st not whom I love
        Alas, thou lov'st not mee.

Seale then this bill of my Divorce to All,
On whom those fainter beames of love did fall;
Marry those loves, which in youth scattered bee
On Fame, Wit, Hopes (false mistresses) to thee.
Churches are best for Prayer, that have least light:
To see God only, I goe out of sight:
    And to scape stormy dayes, I chuse
        An Everlasting night.

Hymne to God my God, in my Sicknesse

Since I am comming to that Holy roome,
    Where, with thy Quire of Saints for evermore,
I shall be made thy Musique; As I come
    I tune the Instrument here at the dore,
    And what I must doe then, thinke here before.

Whilst my Physitians by their love are growne
    Cosmographers, and I their Mapp, who lie
Flat on this bed, that by them may be showne
    That this is my South-west discoverie
    Per fretum febris, by these streights to die,

I joy, that in these straits, I see my West;
    For, though theire currants yeeld returne to none,
What shall my West hurt me? As West and East
    In all flatt Maps (and I am one) are one,
    So death doth touch the Resurrection.

Is the Pacifique Sea my home? Or are
    The Easterne riches? Is Jerusalem?
Anyan, and Magellan, and Gibraltare,
    All streights, and none but streights, are wayes to them,
    Whether where Japhet dwelt, or Cham, or Sem.

We thinke that Paradise and Calvarie,
   Christs Crosse, and Adams tree, stood in one place;
Looke Lord, and finde both Adams met in me;
   As the first Adams sweat surrounds my face,
   May the last Adams blood my soule embrace.

So, in his purple wrapp'd receive mee Lord,
   By these his thornes give me his other Crowne;
And as to others soules I preach'd thy word,
   Be this my Text, my Sermon to mine owne,
   Therfore that he may raise the Lord throws down.

A Hymne to God the Father

I

Wilt thou forgive that sinne where I begunne,
   Which was my sin, though it were done before?
Wilt thou forgive that sinne; through which I runne,
   And do run still: though still I do deplore?
     When thou hast done, thou hast not done,
       For, I have more.

II

Wilt thou forgive that sinne which I have wonne
   Others to sinne? and, made my sinne their doore?
Wilt thou forgive that sinne which I did shunne
   A yeare, or two: but wallowed in, a score?
     When thou hast done, thou hast not done,
       For I have more.

III

I have a sinne of feare, that when I have spunne
   My last thred, I shall perish on the shore;
But sweare by thy selfe, that at my death thy sonne
   Shall shine as he shines now, and heretofore;
     And, having done that, Thou hast done,
       I feare no more.

BEN JONSON 1573?–1637

A Hymne to God the Father

Heare mee, O God!
  A broken heart,
  Is my best part:
Use still thy rod
  That I may prove
  Therein, thy Love.

If thou hadst not
  Beene sterne to mee,
  But left me free,
I had forgot
  My selfe and thee.

For, sin's so sweet,
  As minds ill bent
  Rarely repent,
Untill they meet
  Their punishment.

Who more can crave
  Than thou hast done?
  That gav'st a Sonne,
To free a slave,
  First made of nought;
  With all since bought.

Sinne, Death, and Hell,
  His glorious Name
  Quite overcame,
Yet I rebell,
  And slight the same.

But, I'le come in,
  Before my losse
  Me farther tosse,
As sure to win
  Under his Crosse.

To Celia

Drinke to me, onely, with thine eyes,
    And I will pledge with mine;
Or leave a kisse but in the cup,
    And I'll not looke for wine.
The thirst, that from the soule doth rise,
    Doth aske a drink divine:
But might I of Jove's Nectar sup,
    I would not change for thine.
I sent thee, late, a rosie wreath,
    Not so much honoring thee,
As giving it a hope, that there
    It could not withered bee.
But thou thereon did'st onely breath,
    And sent'st it backe to mee:
Since when it growes, and smells, I sweare,
    Not of it selfe, but thee.

Simplex Munditiis

Still to be neat, still to be drest,
As you were going to a feast;
Still to be powdred, still perfum'd:
Lady, it is to be presum'd,
Though Arts hid causes are not found,
All is not sweet, all is not sound.

Give me a look, give me a face
That makes simplicity a grace;
Robes loosely flowing, hayre as free:
Such sweet neglect more taketh me,
Than all th' adulteries of Art;
They strike mine eyes, but not my heart.

EDWARD, LORD HERBERT
OF CHERBURY
1583–1648

To his Watch, when he could not sleep

Uncessant Minutes, whil'st you move you tell
  The time that tells our life, which though it run
  Never so fast or farr, your new begun
Short steps shall overtake; for though life well

May scape his own Account, it shall not yours,
  You are Death's Auditors, that both divide
  And summ what ere that life inspir'd endures
Past a beginning, and through you we bide

The doom of Fate, whose unrecall'd Decree
  You date, bring, execute; making what's new,
  Ill and good, old, for as we die in you,
You die in Time, Time in Eternity.

Elegy over a Tomb

Must I then see, alas! eternal night
  Sitting upon those fairest eyes,
And closing all those beams, which once did rise
  So radiant and bright,
That light and heat in them to us did prove
  Knowledge and Love?

Oh, if you did delight no more to stay
  Upon this low and earthly stage,

But rather chose an endless heritage,
    Tell us at least, we pray,
Where all the beauties that those ashes ow'd
    Are now bestow'd?

Doth the Sun now his light with yours renew?
    Have Waves the curling of your hair?
Did you restore unto the Sky and Air,
    The red, and white, and blew?
Have you vouchsaf'd to flowers since your death
    That sweetest breath?

Had not Heav'ns Lights else in their houses slept,
    Or to some private life retir'd?
Must not the Sky and Air have else conspir'd,
    And in their Regions wept?
Must not each flower else the earth could breed
    Have been a weed?

But thus enrich'd may we not yield some cause
    Why they themselves lament no more?
That must have chang'd the course they held before,
    And broke their proper Laws,
Had not your beauties giv'n this second birth
    To Heaven and Earth?

Tell us, for Oracles must still ascend,
    For those that crave them at your tomb:
Tell us, where are those beauties now become,
    And what they now intend:
Tell us, alas, that cannot tell our grief,
    Or hope relief.

Sonnet of Black Beauty

Black beauty, which above that common light,
    Whose Power can no colours here renew
    But those which darkness can again subdue,
Dost still remain unvary'd to the sight,
And like an object equal to the view,
    Art neither chang'd with day, nor hid with night;
    When all these colours which the world call bright,
    And which old Poetry doth so persue,
Are with the night so perished and gone,
    That of their being there remains no mark,
Thou still abidest so intirely one,
    That we may know thy blackness is a spark
Of light inaccessible, and alone
    Our darkness which can make us think it dark.

HENRY KING
1592–1669

Sonnet

Tell me no more how fair she is,
   I have no minde to hear
The story of that distant bliss
   I never shall come near:
By sad experience I have found
That her perfection is my wound.

And tell me not how fond I am
   To tempt a daring Fate,
From whence no triumph ever came,
   But to repent too late:
There is some hope ere long I may
In silence dote my self away.

I ask no pity (Love) from thee,
   Nor will thy justice blame,
So that thou wilt not envy mee
   The glory of my flame:
Which crowns my heart when ere it dyes,
In that it falls her sacrifice.

The Exequy

Accept thou Shrine of my dead Saint,
Instead of Dirges this complaint;
And for sweet flowres to crown thy hearse,
Receive a strew of weeping verse
From thy griev'd friend, whom thou might'st see
Quite melted into tears for thee.

Dear loss! since thy untimely fate
My task hath been to meditate
On thee, on thee: thou art the book,
The library whereon I look
Though almost blind. For thee (lov'd clay)
I languish out, not live the day,
Using no other exercise
But what I practise with mine eyes:
By which wet glasses I find out
How lazily time creeps about
To one that mourns: this, onely this
My exercise and bus'ness is:
So I compute the weary houres
With sighs dissolved into showres.

Nor wonder if my time go thus
Backward and most preposterous;
Thou hast benighted me, thy set
This Eve of blackness did beget,
Who wast my day, (though overcast
Before thou had'st thy Noon-tide past)
And I remember must in tears,
Thou scarce had'st seen so many years
As Day tells houres. By thy cleer Sun
My love and fortune first did run;
But thou wilt never more appear
Folded within my Hemisphear,
Since both thy light and motion
Like a fled Star is fall'n and gon,
And twixt me and my soules dear wish

The earth now interposed is,
Which such a strange eclipse doth make
As ne'er was read in Almanake.

   I could allow thee for a time
To darken me and my sad Clime,
Were it a month, a year, or ten,
I would thy exile live till then;
And all that space my mirth adjourn,
So thou wouldst promise to return;
And putting off thy ashy shrowd
At length disperse this sorrows cloud.

   But woe is me! the longest date
Too narrow is to calculate
These empty hopes: never shall I
Be so much blest as to descry
A glimpse of thee, till that day come
Which shall the earth to cinders doome,
And a fierce Feaver must calcine
The body of this world like thine,
(My Little World!); that fit of fire
Once off, our bodies shall aspire
To our soules bliss: then we shall rise,
And view our selves with cleerer eyes
In that calm Region, where no night
Can hide us from each others sight.

   Mean time, thou hast her, earth: much good
May my harm do thee. Since it stood
With Heavens will I might not call
Her longer mine, I give thee all
My short-liv'd right and interest
In her, whom living I lov'd best:
With a most free and bounteous grief,
I give thee what I could not keep.
Be kind to her, and prethee look
Thou write into thy Dooms-day book
Each parcell of this Rarity
Which in thy Casket shrin'd doth ly:
See that thou make thy reck'ning streight,

And yield her back again by weight;
For thou must audit on thy trust
Each graine and atome of this dust,
As thou wilt answer Him that lent,
Not gave thee, my dear Monument.

So close the ground, and 'bout her shade
Black curtains draw, my Bride is laid.

Sleep on my Love in thy cold bed
Never to be disquieted!
My last good night! Thou wilt not wake
Till I thy fate shall overtake:
Till age, or grief, or sickness must
Marry my body to that dust
It so much loves; and fill the room
My heart keeps empty in thy Tomb.
Stay for me there; I will not faile
To meet thee in that hollow Vale.
And think not much of my delay;
I am already on the way,
And follow thee with all the speed
Desire can make, or sorrows breed.
Each minute is a short degree,
And ev'ry houre a step towards thee.
At night when I betake to rest,
Next morn I rise neerer my West
Of life, almost by eight houres saile,
Than when sleep breath'd his drowsie gale.

Thus from the Sun my Bottom stears,
And my dayes Compass downward bears:
Nor labour I to stemme the tide
Through which to Thee I swiftly glide.

'Tis true, with shame and grief I yield,
Thou like the Van first took'st the field,
And gotten hast the victory
In thus adventuring to dy
Before me, whose more years might crave
A just precedence in the grave.
But heark! My Pulse like a soft Drum

Beats my approach, tells Thee I come;
And slow howe'er my marches be,
I shall at last sit down by Thee.

The thought of this bids me go on,
And wait my dissolution
With hope and comfort. Dear (forgive
The crime) I am content to live
Divided, with but half a heart,
Till we shall meet and never part.

Sic Vita

Like to the falling of a Starre;
Or as the flights of Eagles are;
Or like the fresh springs gawdy hew;
Or silver drops of morning dew;
Or like a wind that chafes the flood;
Or bubbles which on water stood;
Even such is man, whose borrow'd light
Is straight call'd in, and paid to night.

    The Wind blowes out; the Bubble dies;
    The Spring entomb'd in Autumn lies;
    The Dew dries up; the Starre is shot;
    The Flight is past; and Man forgot.

The Surrender

My once dear Love! hapless that I no more
Must call thee so – the rich affection's store
That fed our hopes, lies now exhaust and spent,
Like sums of treasure unto bankrupts lent.
We that did nothing study but the way
To love each other, with which thoughts the day
Rose with delight to us, and with them set,

Must learn the hateful art, how to forget.
We, that did nothing wish that Heaven could give,
Beyond ourselves, nor did desire to live
Beyond that wish, all these now cancel must,
As if not writ in faith, but words and dust.
Yet witness those clear vows which lovers make,
Witness the chaste desires that never brake
Into unruly heats; witness that breast,
Which in thy bosom anchored his whole rest,
'Tis no default in us, I dare acquite
Thy maiden faith, thy purpose fair and white
As thy pure self. Cross planets did envy
Us to each other, and Heaven did untie
Faster than vows could bind. Oh, that the stars,
When lovers meet, should stand opposed in wars!
Since then some higher Destinies command,
Let us not strive, nor labour to withstand
What is past help. The longest date of grief
Can never yield a hope of our relief;
And though we waste ourselves in moist laments,
Tears may drown us, but not our discontents.
Fold back our arms; take home our fruitless loves,
That must new fortunes try, like turtle doves
Dislodgèd from their haunts. We must in tears
Unwind a love knit up in many years.
In this last kiss I here surrender thee
Back to thyself – so thou again art free;
Thou in another, sad as that, re-send
The truest heart that lover e'er did lend.
Now turn from each. So fare our severed hearts,
As the divorced soul from her body parts.

FRANCIS QUARLES
1592–1644

Wherefore hidest thou thy face, and holdest me for thy enemie?

Why dost thou shade thy lovely face? O why
Does that ecclipsing hand, so long, deny
The Sun-shine of thy soule-enliv'ning eye?

Without that Light, what light remaines in me?
Thou art my Life, my Way, my Light; in Thee
I live, I move, and by thy beames I see.

Thou art my Life; If thou but turne away,
My life's a thousand deaths: thou art my Way;
Without thee, Lord, I travell not, but stray.

My Light thou art; without thy glorious sight,
Mine eyes are darkned with perpetuall night.
My God, thou art my Way, my Life, my Light.

Thou art my Way; I wander, if thou flie:
Thou art my Light; if hid, how blind am I!
Thou art my Life; if thou withdraw, I die.

Mine eyes are blind and darke; I cannot see;
To whom, or whither should my darknesse flee,
But to the Light? And who's that Light but Thee?

My path is lost; my wandring steps do stray;
I cannot safely go, nor safely stay;
Whom should I see but Thee, my Path my Way?

O, I am dead: to whom shall I, poore I,
Repaire? to whom shall my sad Ashes fly
But Life? And where is Life but in thine eye?

And yet thou turn'st away thy face, and fly'st me;
And yet I sue for Grace and thou deny'st me;
Speake, art thou angry, Lord, or onely try'st me?

Unskreene those heav'nly lamps, or tell me why
Thou shad'st thy face. Perhaps, thou thinkst, no eye
Can view those flames, and not drop downe and die.

If that be all, shine forth, and draw thee nigher;
Let me behold and die; for my desire
Is Phoenix-like to perish in that Fire.

Death-conquer'd Laz'rus was redeem'd by Thee;
If I am dead, Lord, set death's pris'ner free;
Am I more spent, or stink I worse than he?

If my pufft light be out, give leave to tine
My flameless snuffe at that bright Lamp of thine;
O what's thy Light the lesse for lighting mine?

If I have lost my Path, great Shepheard, say,
Shall I still wander in a doubtfull way?
Lord, shall a Lamb of Isr'el's sheepfold stray?

Thou art the Pilgrim's Path: the blind man's Eye;
The dead man's Life; on thee my hopes rely;
If thou remove, I erre; I grope; I die.

Disclose thy Sun beames; close thy wings, and stay;
See, see, how I am blind, and dead, and stray,
O thou, that art my Light, my Life, my Way.

A Divine Rapture

E'en like two little bank-dividing brooks,
   That wash the pebbles with their wanton streams,
And having ranged and searched a thousand nooks,
   Meet both at length in silver-breasted Thames,
   Where in a greater current they conjoin:
So I my Best-belovèd's am; so He is mine.

E'en so we met and after long pursuit,
   E'en so we joined, we both became entire;
No need for either to renew a suit,
   For I was flax, and He was flames of fire:
   Our firm-united souls did more than twine;
So I my Best-belovèd's am; so He is mine.

If all those glittering Monarchs, that command
   The servile quarters of this earthly ball,
Should tender in exchange their shares of land,
   I would not change my fortunes for them all:
   Their wealth is but a counter to my coin:
The world's but theirs; but my Belovèd's mine.

GEORGE HERBERT
1593–1633

Redemption

Having been tenant long to a rich Lord,
　Not thriving, I resolvèd to be bold,
And make a suit unto Him, to afford
　A new small-rented lease, and cancell th' old.

In heaven at His manour I Him sought:
　They told me there, that He was lately gone
About some land, which he had dearly bought
　Long since on Earth, to take possession.

I straight return'd, and knowing His great birth,
　Sought Him accordingly in great resorts –
　In cities, theatres, gardens, parks, and courts:
At length I heard a ragged noise and mirth

　Of theeves and murderers; there I Him espied,
Who straight, 'Your suit is granted,' said, and died.

Easter

Rise, heart, Thy Lord is risen; sing His praise
                Without delays,
Who takes thee by the hand, that thou likewise
                With Him mayst rise;
That, as His death calcinèd thee to dust,
His life may make thee gold, and, much more, just.

Awake, my lute, and struggle for thy part
                With all thy art:
The crosse taught all wood to resound His name
                Who bore the same;
His stretchèd sinews taught all strings what key
Is best to celebrate this most high day.

Consort both heart and lute, and twist a song
                Pleasant and long;
Or, since all musick is but three parts vied
                And multiplied,
O, let Thy blessèd Spirit bear a part,
And make up our defects with His sweet art.

The Song

I got me flowers to straw Thy way,
I got me boughs off many a tree;
But Thou wast up by break of day,
And brought'st Thy sweets along with Thee.

The sunne arising in the East,
Though he give light, and th' East perfume,
If they should offer to contest
With Thy arising, they presume.

Can there be any day but this,
Though many sunnes to shine endeavour?
We count three hundred, but we misse:
There is but one, and that one ever.

Another version, from the Williams MS

I had preparèd many a flowre
To strow Thy way and victorie;
But Thou wast up before myne houre,
Bringing Thy sweets along with Thee.

The sunn arising in the East,
Though hee bring light and th' other sents,
Can not make up so braue a feast
As Thy discouerie presents.

Yet though my flours be lost, they say
A hart can never come too late;
Teach it to sing Thy praise this day,
And then this day my life shall date.

Easter Wings

Lord, Who createdst man in wealth and store,
    Though foolishly he lost the same,
        Decaying more and more,
            Till he became
                Most poore:
                With Thee
            O let me rise,
        As larks, harmoniously,
    And sing this day Thy victories:
Then shall the fall further the flight in me.

My tender age in sorrow did beginne;
    And still with sicknesses and shame
        Thou didst so punish sinne,
            That I became
                Most thinne.
                With Thee
            Let me combine,
        And feel this day Thy victorie;
    For, if I imp my wing on Thine,
Affliction shall advance the flight in me.

Affliction

When first Thou didst entice to Thee my heart,
           I thought the service brave:
So many joyes I writ down for my part,
           Besides what I might have
Out of my stock of naturall delights,
Augmented with Thy gracious benefits.

I lookèd on Thy furniture so fine,
           And made it fine to me;
Thy glorious houshold-stuffe did me entwine,
           And 'tice me unto Thee;
Such starres I counted mine: both heav'n and earth
Payd me my wages in a world of mirth.

What pleasures could I want, whose King I served,
           Where joyes my fellows were?
Thus argu'd into hopes, my thoughts reserved
           No place for grief or fear;
Therefore my sudden soul caught at the place,
And made her youth and fiercenesse seek Thy face.

At first thou gav'st me milk and sweetnesses,
           I had my wish and way;
My days were straw'd with flow'rs and happinesses;
           There was no moneth but May.
But with my yeares sorrow did twist and grow,
And made a partie unawares for wo.

My flesh began unto my soul in pain,
           Sicknesses cleave my bones,
Consuming agues dwell in ev'ry vein,
           And tune my breath to grones:
Sorrow was all my soul; I scarce beleeved,
Till grief did tell me roundly, that I lived.

When I got health, Thou took'st away my life,
          And more, – for my friends die:
My mirth and edge was lost, a blunted knife
          Was of more use then I:
Thus thinne and lean, without a fence or friend,
I was blown through with ev'ry storm and winde.

Whereas my birth and spirit rather took
          The way that takes the town,
Thou didst betray me to a lingring book,
          And wrap me in a gown;
I was entangled in the world of strife
Before I had the power to change my life.

Yet, for I threatned oft the siege to raise,
          Not simpring all mine age,
Thou often didst with academick praise
          Melt and dissolve my rage:
I took Thy sweetened pill till I came neare;
I could not go away, nor persevere.

Yet lest perchance I should too happie be
          In my unhappinesse,
Turning my purge to food, Thou throwest me
          Into more sicknesses:
Thus doth Thy power cross-bias me, not making
Thine own gift good, yet me from my ways taking.

Now I am here, what Thou wilt do with me
          None of my books will show:
I reade, and sigh, and wish I were a tree, –
          For sure then I should grow
To fruit or shade; at least some bird would trust
Her houshold to me, and I should be just.

Yet, though Thou troublest me, I must be meek;
          In weaknesse must be stout.
Well, I will change the service, and go seek
          Some other master out.
Ah, my deare God, though I am clean forgot,
Let me not love Thee, if I love Thee not.

The Temper

How should I praise Thee, Lord? how should my rymes
   Gladly engrave Thy love in steel,
   If, what my soul doth feel sometimes,
     My soul might ever feel!

Although there were some fourtie heav'ns or more,
   Sometimes I peere above them all;
   Sometimes I hardly reach a score,
     Sometimes to Hell I fall.

O, rack me not to such a vast extent,
   Those distances belong to Thee;
   The world's too little for Thy tent,
     A grave too big for me.

Wilt Thou meet arms with man, that Thou dost stretch
   A crumme of dust from heav'n to hell?
   Will great God measure with a wretch?
     Shall he Thy stature spell?

O, let me, when Thy roof my soul hath hid,
   O, let me roost and nestle there;
   Then of a sinner Thou art rid,
     And I of hope and fear.

Yet take Thy way; for sure Thy way is best:
   Stretch or contract me, Thy poore debter;
   This is but tuning of my breast,
     To make the musick better.

Whether I flie with angels, fall with dust,
   Thy hands made both, and I am there;
   Thy power and love, my love and trust,
     Make one place ev'rywhere.

Jordan

Who says that fictions onely and false hair
Become a verse? Is there in truth no beautie?
Is all good structure in a winding-stair?
May no lines passe, except they do their dutie
    Not to a true, but painted chair?

Is it no verse, except enchanted groves
And sudden arbours shadow coarse-spunne lines?
Must purling streams refresh a lover's loves?
Must all be vail'd while he that reades divines,
    Catching the sense at two removes?

Shepherds are honest people, let them sing:
Riddle who list, for me, and pull for prime,
I envie no man's nightingale or spring;
Nor let them punish me with loss of rhyme,
    Who plainly say, My God, my King.

Prayer

Prayer, the Churche's banquet, Angels' age,
    God's breath in man returning to his birth,
The soul in paraphrase, heart in pilgrimage,
    The Christian plummet sounding heav'n and earth;

Engine against th' Almightie, sinner's towre,
    Reversèd thunder, Christ-side-piercing spear,
The six-daies-world transposing in an houre,
    A kinde of tune which all things heare and fear;

Softnesse, and peace, and joy, and love, and blisse,
    Exalted manna, gladnesse of the best,
    Heaven in ordinarie, man well drest,
The milkie way, the bird of Paradise,

    Church-bels beyond the stars heard, the soul's bloud,
    The land of spices, something understood.

Deniall

When my devotions could not pierce
    Thy silent eares,
Then was my heart broken, as was my verse;
  My breast was full of fears
    And disorder;

My bent thoughts, like a brittle bow,
    Did flie asunder;
Each took his way; some would to pleasures go,
  Some to the warres and thunder
    Of alarms.

As good go any where, they say,
    As to benumme
Both knees and heart in crying night and day,
  'Come, come, my God, O come!'
    But no hearing.

O that Thou shouldst give dust a tongue
    To crie to Thee,
And then not hear it crying! All day long
  My heart was in my knee,
    But no hearing.

Therefore my soul lay out of sight,
    Untun'd, unstrung;
My feeble spirit, unable to look right,
  Like a nipt blossome, hung
    Discontented.

O, cheer and tune my heartlesse breast,
    Deferre no time;
That so Thy favours granting my request,
  They and my minde may chime,
    And mend my ryme.

Vanitie

The fleet astronomer can bore
And thred the spheres with his quick-piercing minde;
He views their stations, walks from doore to doore,
    Surveys as if he had design'd
To make a purchase there; he sees their dances,
    And knoweth long before
Both their full-ey'd aspécts and secret glances.

The nimble diver with his side
Cuts through the working waves, that he may fetch
His dearly-earnèd pearl; which God did hide
    On purpose from the venturous wretch,
That He might save his life, and also hers
    Who with excessive pride
Her own destruction and his danger wears.

The subtil chymick can devest
And strip the creature naked, till he finde
The callow principles within their nest:
    There he imparts to them his minde,
Admitted to their bed-chamber before
    They appeare trim and drest
To ordinarie suitours at the doore.

What hath not man sought out and found,
But his deare God? Who yet His glorious law
Embosomes in us, mellowing the ground
    With showers and frosts, with love and aw,
So that we need not say, Where's this command?
    Poore man, thou searchest round
To find out death, but missest life at hand!

The Pearl

MATTHEW 13: 45

I know the wayes of Learning; both the head
And pipes that feed the presse, and make it runne;
What Reason hath from Nature borrowèd,
Or of itself, like a good huswife, spunne
In laws and policie; what the starres conspire,
What willing Nature speaks, what forc'd by fire;
Both th' old discoveries and the new-found seas,
The stock and surplus, cause and historie, –
All these stand open, or I have the keyes:
        Yet I love Thee.

I know the wayes of Honour, what maintains
The quick returns of courtesie and wit;
In vies of favours whether partie gains;
When glorie swells the heart, and moldeth it
To all expressions both of hand and eye;
Which on the world a true-love knot may tie,
And bear the bundle, wheresoe're it goes;
How many drammes of spirit there must be
To sell my life unto my friends or foes:
        Yet I love Thee.

I know the wayes of pleasure, the sweet strains,
The lullings and the relishes of it;
The propositions of hot bloud and brains;
What mirth and musick mean; what Love and Wit
Have done these twentie hundred years and more;
I know the projects of unbridled store:
My stuffe is flesh, not brasse; my senses live,
And grumble oft that they have more in me
Then He that curbs them, being but one to five:
        Yet I love Thee.

I know all these, and have them in my hand:
Therefore not seelèd, but with open eyes
I flie to Thee, and fully understand

Both the main sale and the commodities;
And at what rate and price I have Thy love,
With all the circumstances that may move:
Yet through the labyrinths, not my groveling wit,
But Thy silk-twist let down from heav'n to me,
Did both conduct and teach me how by it
                    To climb to Thee.

Life

I made a posie while the day ran by:
Here will I smell my remnant out, and tie
        My life within this band;
But Time did becken to the flow'rs, and they
By noon most cunningly did steal away,
        And wither'd in my hand.

My hand was next to them, and then my heart;
I took, without more thinking, in good part
        Time's gentle admonition;
Who did so sweetly Death's sad taste convey,
Making my minde to smell my fatall day,
        Yet sugring the suspicion.

Farewell, deare flow'rs; sweetly your time ye spent,
Fit while ye lived for smell or ornament,
        And after death for cures.
I follow straight, without complaints or grief;
Since if my scent be good, I care not if
        It be as short as yours.

Mortification

How soon doth man decay!
When clothes are taken from a chest of sweets
   To swaddle infants, whose young breath
      Scarce knows the way,
   Those clouts are little winding-sheets,
Which do consign and send them unto Death.

   When boyes go first to bed,
They step into their voluntarie graves;
   Sleep binds them fast, onely their breath
      Makes them not dead:
   Successive nights, like rolling waves,
Convey them quickly who are bound for Death.

   When Youth is frank and free,
And calls for musick, while his veins do swell,
   All day exchanging mirth and breath
      In companie,
   That musick summons to the knell
Which shall befriend him at the house of Death.

   When man grows staid and wise,
Getting a house and home, where he may move
   Within the circle of his breath,
      Schooling his eyes,
   That dumbe inclosure maketh love
Unto the coffin that attends his death.

   When Age grows low and weak,
Marking his grave, and thawing ev'ry year,
   Till all do melt and drown his breath
      When he would speak,
   A chair or litter shows the biere
Which shall convey him to the house of Death.

Man, ere he is aware,
Hath put together a solemnitie,
And drest his hearse, while he has breath
As yet to spare;
Yet, Lord, instruct us so to die,
That all these dyings may be LIFE in DEATH.

The Collar

I struck the board, and cry'd, 'No more;
I will abroad.'
What, shall I ever sigh and pine?
My lines and life are free; free as the road,
Loose as the winde, as large as store.
Shall I be still in suit?
Have I no harvest but a thorn
To let me bloud, and not restore
What I have lost with cordiall fruit?
Sure there was wine
Before my sighs did drie it; there was corn
Before my tears did drown it;
Is the yeare onely lost to me?
Have I no bayes to crown it,
No flowers, no garlands gay? all blasted,
All wasted?
Not so, my heart; but there is fruit,
And thou hast hands.
Recover all thy sigh-blown age
On double pleasures; leave thy cold dispute
Of what is fit and not; forsake thy cage,
Thy rope of sands
Which pettie thoughts have made; and made to thee
Good cable, to enforce and draw,
And be thy law,
While thou didst wink and wouldst not see.
Away! take heed;
I will abroad.

Call in thy death's-head there, tie up thy fears;
> He that forbears
>> To suit and serve his need
>>> Deserves his load.
But as I rav'd and grew more fierce and wilde
>> At every word,
>> Methought I heard one calling, 'Childe';
>>> And I reply'd, 'My Lord.'

The Pulley

When God at first made man,
Having a glasse of blessings standing by,
'Let us,' said He, 'poure on him all we can;
Let the world's riches, which dispersèd lie,
>>> Contract into a span.'

So strength first made a way;
Then beautie flow'd, then wisdome, honour, pleasure;
When almost all was out, God made a stay,
Perceiving that, alone of all His treasure,
>>> Rest in the bottome lay.

'For if I should,' said He,
'Bestow this jewell also on My creature,
He would adore My gifts in stead of Me,
And rest in Nature, not the God of Nature:
>>> So both should losers be.

'Yet let him keep the rest,
But keep them with repining restlessnesse;
Let him be rich and wearie, that at least,
If goodnesse leade him not, yet wearinesse
>>> May tosse him to My breast.'

Discipline

Throw away Thy rod,
Throw away Thy wrath;
                    O my God,
Take the gentle path.

For my heart's desire
Unto Thine is bent;
                    I aspire
To a full consent.

Nor a word or look
I affect to own,
                    But by book,
And Thy Book alone.

Though I fail, I weep;
Though I halt in pace,
                    Yet I creep
To the throne of grace.

Then let wrath remove,
Love will do the deed;
                    For with love
Stonie hearts will bleed.

Love is swift of foot;
Love's a man of warre,
                    And can shoot,
And can hit from farre.

Who can scape his bow?
That which wrought on Thee,
                    Brought Thee low,
Needs must work on me.

Throw away Thy rod:
Though man frailties hath,
                    Thou art God;
Throw away Thy wrath.

Death

Death, thou wast once an uncouth hideous thing,
           Nothing but bones,
        The sad effect of sadder grones:
Thy mouth was open, but thou couldst not sing.

For we consider'd thee as at some six
                  Or ten yeares hence,
           After the losse of life and sense;
Flesh being turned to dust, and bones to sticks.

We lookt on this side of thee, shooting short,
                  Where we did finde
           The shells of fledge souls left behinde;
Dry dust, which sheds no tears, but may extort.

But since our Saviour's death did put some bloud
                  Into thy face,
           Thou art grown fair and full of grace,
Much in request, much sought for, as a good.

For we do now behold thee gay and glad,
                  As at doom's-day,
           When souls shall wear their new aray,
And all thy bones with beautie shall be clad.

Therefore we can go die as sleep, and trust
                  Half that we have
           Unto an honest faithfull grave,
Making our pillows either down or dust.

The Elixer

Teach me, my God and King,
    In all things Thee to see,
And what I do in any thing
    To do it as for Thee.

Not rudely, as a beast,
    To runne into an action
But still to make Thee prepossest,
    And give it his perfection.

A man that looks on glasse,
    On it may stay his eye;
Or if he pleaseth, through it passe,
    And then the heav'n espie.

All may of Thee partake:
    Nothing can be so mean
Which with his tincture, 'for Thy sake',
    Will not grow bright and clean.

A servant with this clause
    Makes drudgerie divine;
Who sweeps a room as for Thy laws
    Makes that and th' action fine.

This is the famous stone
    That turneth all to gold;
For that which God doth touch and own
    Cannot for lesse be told.

Love

Love bade me welcome; yet my soul drew back,
        Guiltie of dust and sinne.
But quick-ey'd Love, observing me grow slack
        From my first entrance in,
Drew nearer to me, sweetly questioning
        If I lack'd any thing.

'A guest,' I answer'd, 'worthy to be here':
        Love said, 'You shall be he.'
'I, the unkind, ungrateful? Ah, my dear,
        I cannot look on Thee.'
Love took my hand, and smiling did reply,
        'Who made the eyes but I?'

'Truth, Lord; but I have marr'd them; let my shame
        Go where it doth deserve.'
'And know you not,' says Love, 'Who bore the blame?'
        'My dear, then I will serve.'
'You must sit down,' says Love, 'and taste My meat.'
        So I did sit and eat.

THOMAS CAREW
1595–1639

Good Counsell to a Young Maid

Gaze not on thy beauties pride,
Tender Maid, in the false tide
That from Lovers eyes doth slide.

Let thy faithful Chrystall show,
How thy colours come, and goe,
Beautie takes a foyle from woe.

Love, that in those smooth streames lyes,
Under pities faire disguise,
Will thy melting heart surprize.

Nets, of passions finest thred,
Snaring Poems, will be spred,
All, to catch thy maiden-head.

Then beware, for those that cure
Loves disease, themselves endure
For reward a Calenture.

Rather let the Lover pine,
Than his pale cheek should assigne
A perpetuall blush to thine.

An Elegie upon the
Death of the Deane of Pauls,
Dr John Donne

Can we not force from widdowed Poetry,
Now thou art dead (Great DONNE), one Elegie
To crowne thy Hearse? Why yet dare we not trust
Though with unkneaded dowe-bak't prose thy dust,
Such as the uncisor'd Churchman from the flower
Of fading Rhetorique, short liv'd as his houre,
Dry as the sand that measures it, should lay
Upon thy Ashes, on the funerall day?
Have we no voice, no tune? Did'st thou dispense
Through all our language, both the words and sense?
'Tis a sad truth; The Pulpit may her plaine,
And sober Christian precepts still retaine,
Doctrines it may, and wholesome Uses frame,
Grave Homilies, and Lectures, But the flame
Of thy brave Soule, that shot such heat and light,
As burnt our earth, and made our darknesse bright,
Committed holy Rapes upon our Will,
Did through the eye the melting heart distill;
And the deepe knowledge of darke truths so teach,
As sense might judge, what phansie could not reach,
Must be desir'd for ever. So the fire,
That fills with spirit and heat the Delphique quire,
Which kindled first by thy Promethean breath,
Glow'd here a while, lies quench't now in thy death;
The Muses garden with Pedantique weedes
O'erspread, was purg'd by thee; The lazie seeds
Of servile imitation throwne away,
And fresh invention planted, Thou didst pay
The debts of our penurious bankrupt age;
Licentious thefts, that make poetique rage
A Mimique fury, when our soules must bee
Possest, or with Anacreons Extasie,
Or Pindars, not their owne; The subtle cheat
Of slie Exchanges, and the jugling feat

Of two-edg'd words, or whatsoever wrong
By ours was done the Greeke, or Latine tongue,
Thou hast redeem'd, and open'd Us a Mine
Of rich and pregnant phansie, drawne a line
Of masculine expression, which had good
Old Orpheus seene, or all the ancient Brood
Our superstitious fooles admire, and hold
Their lead more precious than thy burnish't Gold,
Thou hadst beene their Exchequer, and no more
They each in others dust had rak'd for Ore.
Thou shalt yield no precedence, but of time,
And the blinde fate of language, whose tun'd chime
More charmes the outward sense; Yet thou maist claime
From so great disadvantage greater fame,
Since to the awe of thy imperious wit
Our stubborne language bends, made only fit
With her tough-thick-rib'd hoopes to gird about
Thy Giant phansie, which had prov'd too stout
For their soft melting Phrases. As in time
They had the start, so did they cull the prime
Buds of invention many a hundred yeare,
And left the rifled fields, besides the feare
To touch their Harvest, yet from those bare lands
Of what is purely thine, thy only hands
(And that thy smallest worke) have gleaned more
Than all those times, and tongues could reape before;
But thou art gone, and thy strict lawes will be
Too hard for Libertines in Poetrie.
They will repeale the goodly exil'd traine
Of gods and goddesses, which in thy just raigne
Were banish'd nobler Poems, now, with these
The silenc'd tales o'th'Metamorphoses
Shall stuffe their lines, and swell the windy Page,
Till Verse refin'd by thee, in this last Age
Turne ballad rime, or those old Idolls bee
Ador'd againe, with new apostasie;
Oh, pardon mee, that breake with untun'd verse
The reverend silence that attends thy herse,
Whose awfull solemne murmures were to thee
More than these faint lines, a loud Elegie,

That did proclaime in a dumbe eloquence
The death of all the Arts, whose influence
Growne feeble, in these panting numbers lies
Gasping short winded Accents, and so dies:
So doth the swiftly turning wheele not stand
In th'instant we withdraw the moving hand,
But some small time maintaine a faint weake course
By vertue of the first impulsive force:
And so whil'st I cast on thy funerall pile
Thy crowne of Bayes, Oh, let it crack a while,
And spit disdaine, till the devouring flashes
Suck all the moysture up, then turne to ashes.
I will not draw thee envy to engrosse
All thy perfections, or weepe all our losse;
Those are too numerous for an Elegie,
And this too great, to be express'd by mee,
Though every pen should share a distinct part.
Yet art thou Theme enough to tire all Art;
Let others carve the rest, it shall suffice
I on thy Tombe this Epitaph incise.

> *Here lies a King, that rul'd as hee thought fit*
> *The universall Monarchy of wit;*
> *Her lie two Flamens, and both those the best,*
> *Apollo's first, at last, the true Gods Priest.*

Mediocritie in Love Rejected

Give me more love, or more disdain;
   The Torrid, or the frozen Zone,
Bring equall ease unto my pain;
   The temperate affords me none:
Either extreame, of love, or hate,
Is sweeter than a calm estate.
Give me a storm: if it be love,
   Like Danaë in that golden showre
I swimme in pleasure; if it prove
   Disdain, that torrent will devoure
My Vulture-hopes; and he's possest
Of Heaven, that's but from Hell releast:
   Then crowne my joys, or cure my pain;
   Give me more love, or more disdaine.

To my Inconstant Mistris

When thou, poore excommunicate
   From all the joyes of love, shalt see
The full reward, and glorious fate,
   Which my strong faith shall purchase me,
Then curse thine owne inconstancy.

A fayrer hand than thine, shall cure
   That heart, which thy false oathes did wound;
And to my soul; a soul more pure
   Than thine, shall by Loves hand be bound,
And both with equall glory crown'd.

Then shalt thou weepe, entreat, complain
   To Love, as I did once to thee;
When all thy teares shall be as vain
   As mine were then, for thou shalt bee
Damn'd for thy false Apostasie.

A Deposition from Love

I was foretold, your rebell sex,
    Nor love, nor pitty knew;
And with what scorn you use to vex
    Poor hearts that humbly sue;
Yet I believ'd, to crown our pain,
    Could we the fortress win,
The happy Lover sure should gain
    A Paradise within:
I thought Loves plagues, like Dragons sate,
Only to fright us at the gate.

But I did enter, and enjoy
    What happy Lovers prove;
For I could kiss, and sport, and toy,
    And taste those sweets of love;
Which had they but a lasting state,
    Or if in Celia's brest
The force of love might not abate,
    Jove were too mean a guest.
But now her breach of faith, farre more
Afflicts, than did her scorn before.

Hard fate! to have been once possest,
    As victor, of a heart
Achiev'd with labour, and unrest,
    And then forc'd to depart.
If the stout Foe will not resigne
    When I besiege a Town,
I lose, but what was never mine;
    But he that is cast down
From enjoy'd beauty, feels a woe
Only deposed Kings can know.

Ingratefull Beauty threatned

Know Celia, (since thou art so proud,)
  'Twas I that gave thee thy renown:
Thou hadst, in the forgotten crowd
  Of common beauties, liv'd unknown,
Had not my verse exhal'd thy name,
And with it impt the wings of fame.

That killing power is none of thine,
  I gave it to thy voyce, and eyes:
Thy sweets, thy graces, all are mine;
  Thou art my star, shin'st in my skies;
Then dart not from thy borrowed sphere
Lightning on him that fixt thee there.

Tempt me with such affrights no more,
  Lest what I made, I uncreate:
Let fools thy mystique forms adore,
  I'll know thee in thy mortall state;
Wise Poets that wrapp'd Truth in tales,
Knew her themselves through all her vailes.

Boldness in Love

Mark how the bashful morn in vain
  Courts the amorous marigold,
With sighing blasts and weeping rain,
  Yet she refuses to unfold.
But when the planet of the day
Approacheth with his powerful ray,
Then she spreads, then she receives
His warmer beams into her virgin leaves.
So shalt thou thrive in love, fond boy;
If thy tears and sighs discover
Thy grief, thou never shalt enjoy

The just reward of a bold lover!
But when with moving accents thou
Shalt constant faith and service vow,
Thy Celia shall receive those charms
With open ears, and with unfolded arms.

A Song

Ask me no more where Jove bestowes,
When June is past, the fading rose:
For in your beauties orient deep,
These Flowers as in their causes sleep.

Ask me no more whither doe stray
The golden Atomes of the day:
For in pure love heaven did prepare
Those powders to inrich your hair.

Ask me no more whither doth hast
The Nightingale, when May is past:
For in your sweet dividing throat
She winters, and keeps warm her note.

Ask me no more where those starres light,
That downwards fall in dead of night:
For in your eyes they sit, and there,
Fixed, become as in their sphere.

Ask me no more if East or West,
The Phenix builds her spicy nest:
For unto you at last she flyes,
And in your fragrant bosome dies.

To a Lady that desired I would love her

Now you have freely given me leave to love,
    What will you do?
  Shall I your mirth, or passion move,
    When I begin to woo;
Will you torment, or scorn, or love me too?

Each petty beauty can disdain, and I
    Spight of your hate
  Without your leave can see, and die;
    Dispence a nobler Fate!
'Tis easie to destroy, you may create.

Then give me leave to love, & love me too
    Not with designe
  To raise, as Loves curst Rebels doe,
    When puling Poets whine,
Fame to their beauty, from their blubbr'd eyn.

Grief is a puddle, and reflects not clear
    Your beauties rayes;
  Joyes are pure streames, your eyes appear
    Sullen in sadder layes;
In cheerfull numbers they shine bright with prayse,

Which shall not mention to express you fayr,
    Wounds, flames, and darts,
  Storms in your brow, nets in your hair,
    Suborning all your parts,
Or to betray, or torture captive hearts.

I'll make your eyes like morning Suns appear,
    As mild, and fair;
  Your brow as Crystall smooth, and clear,
    And your dishevell'd hair
Shall flow like a calm Region of the Air.

Rich Nature's store, (which is the Poet's Treasure)
    I'll spend, to dress
  Your beauties, if your mine of Pleasure
    In equall thankfulness
You but unlock, so we each other bless.

SIR WILLIAM DAVENANT
1605–1668

Morning

The lark now leaves his wat'ry nest,
   And climbing shakes his dewy wings,
He takes this window for the east,
   And to implore your light he sings –
Awake, awake! the morn will never rise
Till she can dress her beauty at your eyes.

The merchant bows unto the seaman's star,
   The ploughman from the sun his seasons takes:
But still the lover wonders what they are,
   Who look for day before his mistress wakes.
Awake, awake! break through your veil of lawn!
Then draw your curtains and begin the dawn.

EDMUND WALLER
1606–1687

The Selfe-banished

It is not that I love you less,
Than when before your feet I lay,
But to prevent the sad increase
Of hopeless love, I keep away.

In vaine (alas!) for everything
Which I have knowne belong to you,
Your forme does to my fancy bring,
And make my old wounds bleed anew.

Who in the Spring from the new Sun
Already has a Fever got,
Too late begins these shafts to shun
Which Phœbus through his veines has shot.

Too late he would the paine assuage,
And to thick shadowes does retire;
About with him he beares the rage,
And in his tainted blood the fire.

But vow'd I have, and never must
Your banish'd servant trouble you;
For if I breake, you may mistrust
The vow I made to love you too.

Song

Goe lovely Rose,
Tell her that wastes her time and me,
That now she knowes,
When I resemble her to thee,
How sweet and fair she seems to be.

Tell her that's young,
And shuns to have her graces spied,
That hadst thou sprung
In deserts where no men abide,
Thou must have uncommended died

Small is the worth
Of beauty from the light retir'd:
Bid her come forth,
Suffer her selfe to be desir'd,
And not blush so to be admir'd.

Then die, that she
The common fate of all things rare
May read in thee,
How small a part of time they share,
That are so wondrous sweet and faire.

Of the last Verses in the Book

When we for Age could neither read nor write
The subject made us able to indite.
The Soul with nobler Resolutions deckt,
The Body stooping, does Herself erect:
No Mortal Parts are requisite to raise
Her, that Unbody'd can her Maker praise.

The Seas are quiet, when the Winds give o'er
So calm are we, when Passions are no more:
For then we know how vain it was to boast
Of fleeting Things, so certain to be lost.
Clouds of Affection from our younger Eyes
Conceal that emptiness, which Age descries.

The Soul's dark Cottage, batter'd and decay'd,
Lets in new Light thro' chinks that time has made.
Stronger by weakness, wiser Men become
As they draw near to their Eternal home:
Leaving the old, both Worlds at once they view,
That stand upon the threshold of the New.

JOHN MILTON
1608–1674

On Shakespear. 1630

What needs my Shakespear for his honour'd Bones
The labour of an age in piled Stones,
Or that his hallow'd reliques should be hid
Under a Star-ypointing Pyramid?
Dear son of memory, great heir of Fame,
What need'st thou such weak witnes of thy name?
Thou in our wonder and astonishment
Hast built thy self a live-long Monument.
For whilst to th' shame of slow-endeavouring art,
Thy easie numbers flow, and that each heart
Hath from the leaves of thy unvalu'd Book,
Those Delphick lines with deep impression took,
Then thou our fancy of it self bereaving,
Dost make us Marble with too much conceaving;
And so Sepulcher'd in such pomp dost lie,
That Kings for such a Tomb would wish to die.

On the Morning of Christs Nativity

This is the Month, and this the happy morn
Wherin the Son of Heav'ns eternal King,
Of wedded Maid, and Virgin Mother born,
Our great redemption from above did bring;
For so the holy sages once did sing,
    That he our deadly forfeit should release,
And with his Father work us a perpetual peace.

That glorious Form, that Light unsufferable,
And that far-beaming blaze of Majesty,
Wherwith he wont at Heav'ns high Councel-Table,

To sit the midst of Trinal Unity,
He laid aside; and here with us to be,
     Forsook the Courts of everlasting Day,
And chose with us a darksom House of mortal Clay.

Say Heav'nly Muse, shall not thy sacred vein
Afford a present to the Infant God?
Hast thou no verse, no hymn, or solemn strein,
To welcom him to this his new abode,
Now while the Heav'n by the Suns team untrod,
     Hath took no print of the approching light,
And all the spangled host keep watch in squadrons
     bright?

See how from far upon the Eastern rode
The Star-led Wisards haste with odours sweet,
O run, prevent them with thy humble ode,
And lay it lowly at his blessed feet;
Have thou the honour first, thy Lord to greet,
     And joyn thy voice unto the Angel Quire,
From out his secret Altar toucht with hallow'd fire.

The Hymn

It was the Winter wilde,
While the Heav'n-born-childe,
     All meanly wrapt in the rude manger lies;
Nature in aw to him
Had doff't her gawdy trim,
     With her great Master so to sympathize:
It was no season then for her
To wanton with the Sun her lusty Paramour.

Only with speeches fair
She woo's the gentle Air
     To hide her guilty front with innocent Snow,
And on her naked shame,
Pollute with sinfull blame,
     The Saintly Vail of Maiden white to throw,
Confounded, that her Makers eyes
Should look so neer upon her foul deformities.

But he her fears to cease,
Sent down the meek-eyd Peace,
    She crown'd with Olive green, came softly sliding
Down through the turning sphear
His ready Harbinger,
    With Turtle wing the amorous clouds dividing,
And waving wide her mirtle wand,
She strikes a universall Peace through Sea and Land.

No War, or Battails sound
Was heard the World around,
    The idle spear and shield were high up hung;
The hooked Chariot stood
Unstain'd with hostile blood,
    The Trumpet spake not to the armed throng,
And Kings sate still with awfull eye,
As if they surely knew their sovran Lord was by.

But peacefull was the night
Wherin the Prince of light
    His raign of peace upon the earth began:
The Windes with wonder whist,
Smoothly the waters kist,
    Whispering new joyes to the milde Ocean,
Who now hath quite forgot to rave,
While Birds of Calm sit brooding on the charmed wave.

The Stars with deep amaze
Stand fixt in stedfast gaze,
    Bending one way their pretious influence,
And will not take their flight,
For all the morning light,
    Or Lucifer that often warn'd them thence;
But in their glimmering Orbs did glow,
Untill their Lord himself bespake, and bid them go.

And though the shady gloom
Had given day her room,
    The Sun himself with-held his wonted speed,
And hid his head for shame,

As his inferiour flame,
   The new enlightn'd world no more should need;
He saw a greater Sun appear
Than his bright Throne, or burning Axletree could bear.

The Shepherds on the Lawn,
Or ere the point of dawn,
   Sate simply chatting in a rustick row;
Full little thought they than,
That the mighty Pan
   Was kindly com to live with them below;
Perhaps their loves, or els their sheep,
Was all that did their silly thoughts so busie keep.

When such musick sweet
Their hearts and ears did greet,
   As never was by mortall finger strook,
Divinely-warbled voice
Answering the stringed noise,
   As all their souls in blisfull rapture took:
The Air such pleasure loth to lose,
With thousand echo's still prolongs each heav'nly close.

Nature that heard such sound
Beneath the hollow round
   Of Cynthia's seat, the Airy region thrilling,
Now was almost won
To think her part was don,
   And that her raign had here its last fulfilling;
She knew such harmony alone
Could hold all Heav'n and Earth in happier union.

At last surrounds their sight
A Globe of circular light,
   That with long beams the shame-fac't night array'd,
The helmed Cherubim
And sworded Seraphim,
   Are seen in glittering ranks with wings displaid,
Harping in loud and solemn quire,
With unexpressive notes to Heav'ns new-born Heir.

Such Musick (as 'tis said)
Before was never made,
   But when of old the sons of morning sung,
While the Creator Great
His constellations set,
   And the well-ballanc't world on hinges hung,
And cast the dark foundations deep,
And bid the weltring waves their oozy channel keep.

Ring out ye Crystall sphears,
Once bless our human ears,
   (If ye have power to touch our senses so)
And let your silver chime
Move in melodious time;
   And let the Base of Heav'ns deep Organ blow,
And with your ninefold harmony
Make up full consort to th'Angelike symphony.

For if such holy Song
Enwrap our fancy long,
   Time will run back, and fetch the age of gold,
And speckl'd vanity
Will sicken soon and die,
   And leprous sin will melt from earthly mould,
And Hell it self will pass away,
And leave her dolorous mansions to the peering day.

Yea Truth, and Justice then
Will down return to men,
   Th' enameld Arras of the Rain-bow wearing,
And Mercy set between,
Thron'd in Celestiall sheen,
   With radiant feet the tissued clouds down stearing,
And Heav'n as at som festivall,
Will open wide the Gates of her high Palace Hall.

But wisest Fate sayes no,
This must not yet be so,
   The Babe lies yet in smiling Infancy,
That on the bitter cross

Must redeem our loss;
   So both himself and us to glorifie:
Yet first to those ychain'd in sleep,
The wakefull trump of doom must thunder through
    the deep,

With such a horrid clang
As on mount Sinai rang
   While the red fire, and smouldring clouds out brake:
The aged Earth agast
With terrour of that blast,
   Shall from the surface to the center shake;
When at the worlds last session,
The dreadfull Judge in middle Air shall spread his
    throne.

And then at last our bliss
Full and perfect is,
   But now begins; for from this happy day
Th'old Dragon under ground
In straiter limits bound,
   Not half so far casts his usurped sway,
And wrath to see his Kingdom fail,
Swindges the scaly Horrour of his foulded tail.

The Oracles are dumm,
No voice or hideous humm
   Runs through the arched roof in words deceiving.
Apollo from his shrine
Can no more divine,
   With hollow shreik the steep of Delphos leaving.
No nightly trance, or breathed spell,
Inspire's the pale-ey'd Priest from the prophetic cell.

The lonely mountains o're,
And the resounding shore,
   A voice of weeping heard, and loud lament;
From haunted spring, and dale
Edg'd with poplar pale,
   The parting Genius is with sighing sent,
With flowre-inwov'n tresses torn
The Nimphs in twilight shade of tangled thickets mourn.

In consecrated Earth,
And on the holy Hearth,
    The Lars, and Lemures moan with midnight plaint,
In Urns, and Altars round,
A drear, and dying sound
    Affrights the Flamins at their service quaint;
And the chill Marble seems to sweat,
While each peculiar power forgoes his wonted seat.

Peor, and Baalim,
Forsake their Temples dim,
    With that twice-batter'd god of Palestine,
And mooned Ashtaroth,
Heav'ns Queen and Mother both,
    Now sits not girt with Tapers holy shine,
The Libyc Hammon shrinks his horn,
In vain the Tyrian Maids their wounded Thamuz mourn.

And sullen Moloch fled,
Hath left in shadows dred,
    His burning Idol all of blackest hue,
In vain with Cymbals ring,
They call the grisly king,
    In dismall dance about the furnace blue;
The brutish gods of Nile as fast,
Isis and Orus, and the Dog Anubis hast.

Nor is Osiris seen
In Memphian Grove, or Green,
    Trampling the unshowr'd Grasse with lowings loud:
Nor can he be at rest
Within his sacred chest,
    Naught but profoundest Hell can be his shroud,
In vain with Timbrel'd Anthems dark
The sable-stoled Sorcerers bear his worshipt Ark.

He feels from Juda's Land
The dredded Infants hand,
    The rayes of Bethlehem blind his dusky eyn;
Nor all the gods beside,

Longer dare abide,
    Not Typhon huge ending in snaky twine:
Our Babe to shew his Godhead true,
Can in his swadling bands controul the damned crew.

So when the Sun in bed,
Curtain'd with cloudy red,
    Pillows his chin upon an Orient wave,
The flocking shadows pale,
Troop to th' infernall jail,
    Each fetter'd Ghost slips to his severall grave,
And the yellow-skirted Fayes,
Fly after the Night-steeds, leaving their Moon-lov'd maze.

But see the Virgin blest,
Hath laid her Babe to rest.
    Time is our tedious Song should here have ending,
Heav'ns youngest teemed Star,
Hath fixt her polisht Car,
    Her sleeping Lord with Handmaid Lamp attending:
And all about the Courtly Stable,
Bright-harnest Angels sit in order serviceable.

On his Blindness

When I consider how my light is spent,
    E're half my days, in this dark world and wide,
    And that one Talent which is death to hide,
    Lodg'd with me useless, though my Soul more bent
To serve therewith my Maker, and present
    My true account, least he returning chide,
    Doth God exact day-labour, light deny'd,
    I fondly ask; But patience to prevent
That murmur, soon replies, God doth not need
    Either man's work or his own gifts, who best
    Bear his milde yoak, they serve him best, his State
Is Kingly. Thousands at his bidding speed
    And post o're Land and Ocean without rest:
They also serve who only stand and waite.

SIR JOHN SUCKLING
1609–1642

Why so pale and wan?

Why so pale and wan, fond lover?
  Prethee why so pale?
Will, when looking well can't move her
    Looking ill prevail?
    Prethee why so pale?

Why so dull and mute young sinner?
  Prethee why so mute?
Will, when speaking well can't win her
  ˅ Saying nothing do 't?
    Prethee why so mute?

Quit, quit for shame, this will not move,
    This cannot take her;
If of her self she will not love,
    Nothing can make her:
    The divel take her.

A Doubt of Martyrdom

Oh! for some honest Lovers ghost,
  Some kind unbodied post
  Sent from the shades below.
  I strangely long to know
Whether the nobler Chaplets wear,
Those that their mistresse scorn did bear,
  Or those that were us'd kindly.

For what-so-e'er they tell us here
    To make those sufferings dear,
    'Twill there I fear be found,
    That to the being crown'd
T' have lov'd alone, will not suffice
Unlesse we also have been wise,
    And have our Loves enjoy'd.

What posture can we think him in,
    That here unlov'd agen
    Departs and 's thither gone
    Where each sits by his own?
Or how can that Elizium be
Where I my Mistresse still must see
    Circled in others Armes?

For there the Judges all are just,
    And Sophonisba must
    Be his whom she held dear;
    Not his who lov'd her here:
The sweet Philoclea since she died
Lies by her Pirocles his side,
    Not by Amphialus.

Some Bayes (perchance) or Myrtle bough
    For difference crowns the brow
    Of those kind souls that were
    The noble Martyrs here;
And if that be the onely odds
(As who can tell) ye kinder Gods,
    Give me the Woman here.

The Constant Lover

    Out upon it, I have lov'd,
    Three whole days together;
    And am like to love three more,
    If it prove fair weather.

Time shall moult away his wings
Ere he shall discover
In the whole wide world agen
Such a constant Lover.

But the spite on 't is, no praise
Is due at all to me:
Love with me had made no staies,
Had it any been but she.

Had it any been but she
And that very Face,
There had been at least ere this
A dozen dozen in her place.

Song

No, no, fair Heretick, it needs must be
But an ill love in me,
And worse for Thee;
For were it in my power,
To love thee now this hower
More than I did the last;
I would then so fall
I might not love at all;
Love that can flow, and can admit increase,
Admits as well an ebbe, and may grow lesse.

True Love is still the same; the Torrid Zones,
And those more frigid ones
It must not know:
For love grown cold or hot,
Is lust, or friendship, not
The thing we have.
For that's a flame would dye
Held down, or up too high:
Then think I love more than I can expresse,
And would love more could I but love thee lesse.

RICHARD CRASHAW
1612–49

Charitas Nimia, *or the Dear Bargain*

Lord, what is Man? why should he cost Thee
So dear? what had his ruin lost Thee?
Lord, what is man? that Thou hast over-bought
    So much a thing of nought.

Love is too kind, I see, and can
Make but a simple merchant man.
'Twas for such sorry merchandise,
    Bold painters have put out his eyes.

Alas, sweet Lord, what were't to Thee
If there were no such worms as we?
Heav'n ne'ertheless still Heav'n would be.
    Should mankind dwell
    In the deep Hell
What have *his* woes to do with Thee?

    Let him go weep
    O'er his own wounds:
    Seraphim will not sleep
Nor spheres let fall their faithful rounds
    Still would the youthful Spirits sing,
    And still Thy spacious palace ring;
Still would those beauteous Ministers of light
    Burn all as bright,

And bow their flaming heads before Thee
Still thrones and dominations would adore Thee,
Still would those ever-wakeful sons of fire
    Keep warm Thy praise
    Both nights and days
And teach Thy loved Name to their noble lyre.

Let froward dust then do its kind:
And give itself for sport to the proud wind.
   Why should a piece of peevish clay plead shares
     In the eternity of Thy old cares?
Why should'st Thou bow Thine awful breast to see
   What mine own madnesses have done with me?

   Should not the King still keep His throne
   Because some desperate fool's undone?
Or will the world's illustrious eyes
Weep for every worm that dies?
   Will the gallant Sun
   E'er the less glorious run?
Will he hang down his golden head
Or e'er the sooner seek his Western bed,
   Because some foolish fly
   Grows wanton and will die?

O my Saviour, make me see
How dearly Thou hast paid for me,
That lost again, my life may prove
As then in Death, so now in Love.

An Epitaph upon Husband and Wife, which died, and were buried together

To these, whom Death again did wed,
This grave 's the second Marriage-bed.
For though the hand of Fate could force
'Twixt Soul and Body a Divorce,
It could not sunder man and wife,
'Cause they both lived but one life.
Peace, good Reader. Doe not weep.
Peace, the Lovers are asleep.
They, sweet Turtles, folded lie
In the last knot Love could tie.
And though they lie as they were dead,
Their pillow stone, their sheetes of lead
(Pillow hard, and sheets not warm)
Love made the bed; they'll take no harm.
Let them sleep: let them sleep on,
Till this stormy night be gone,
Till the Æternal morrow dawn;
Then the curtaines will be drawn
And they wake into a light
Whose day shall never die in Night.

ABRAHAM COWLEY
1618–67

Drinking

The thirsty Earth soaks up the Rain,
And drinks and gapes for drink again.
The Plants suck in the Earth, and are
With constant drinking fresh and faire.
The Sea it self, which one would think
Should have but little need of Drink,
Drinks ten thousand Rivers up,
So fill'd that they oreflow the Cup.
The busie Sun (and one would guess
By's drunken fiery face no less)
Drinks up the Sea, and when h'as done,
The Moon and Stars drink up the Sun.
They drink and dance by their own light,
They drink and revel all the night.
Nothing in Nature's Sober found,
But an eternal Health goes round.
Fill up the Bowl, then fill it high,
Fill all the Glasses there, For why
Should every creature drink but I,
Why, Man of Morals, tell me why?

RICHARD LOVELACE
1618–57

To Lucasta:
Going to the Warres

Tell me not (Sweet) I am unkinde,
  That from the Nunnerie
Of thy chaste breast, and quiet minde,
  To Warre and Armes I flie.

True; a new Mistresse now I chase,
  The first Foe in the Field;
And with a stronger Faith imbrace
  A Sword, a Horse, a Shield.

Yet this Inconstancy is such,
  As you too shall adore;
I could not love thee (Deare) so much,
  Lov'd I not Honour more.

The Scrutinie

Why should you sweare I am forsworn,
    Since thine I vow'd to be?
Lady it is already Morn,
    And 'twas last night I swore to thee
That fond impossibility.

Have I not lov'd thee much and long,
    A tedious twelve houres space?
I must all other Beauties wrong,
    And rob thee of a new imbrace;
Could I still dote upon thy Face.

Not, but all joy in thy browne haire,
    By others may be found;
But I must search the black and faire,
    Like skilfull Minerallists that sound
For Treasure in un-plow'd-up ground.

Then, if when I have lov'd my round,
    Thou prov'st the pleasant she;
With spoyles of meaner Beauties crown'd,
    I laden will returne to thee,
Ev'n sated with Varietie.

ANDREW MARVELL
1621–1678

Bermudas

Where the remote Bermudas ride,
In th' Oceans bosom unespy'd,
From a small Boat, that row'd along,
The listening Winds receiv'd this Song:
   What should we do but sing His Praise,
That led us through the watery Maze,
Unto an Isle so long unknown,
And yet far kinder than our own?
Where He the huge Sea-Monsters wracks,
That lift the Deep upon their Backs;
He lands us on a grassy Stage,
Safe from the Storms, and Prelat's rage.
He gave us this eternal Spring,
Which here enamells every thing,
And sends the Fowls to us in care,
On daily Visits through the Air;
He hangs in shades the Orange bright,
Like golden Lamps in a green Night,
And does in the Pomegranates close
Jewels more rich than Ormus shows;
He makes the Figs our mouths to meet,
And throws the Melons at our feet;
But Apples plants of such a price,
No Tree could ever bear them twice;
With Cedars chosen by His hand,
From Lebanon, He stores the Land,
And makes the hollow Seas, that roar,
Proclaime the Ambergris on shoar;
He cast (of which we rather boast)
The Gospel's Pearl upon our Coast,
And in these Rocks for us did frame
A Temple where to sound His Name.
Oh! let our Voice His Praise exalt,

Till it arrive at Heaven's Vault,
Which, thence (perhaps) rebounding, may
Echo beyond the Mexique Bay.
   Thus sung they, in the English boat,
An holy and a chearful Note;
And all the way, to guide their Chime,
With falling Oars they kept the time.

To his Coy Mistress

Had we but World enough, and Time,
This coyness, Lady, were no crime.
We would sit down, and think which way
To walk, and pass our long Loves Day.
Thou by the Indian Ganges side
Should'st rubies find: I by the tide
Of Humber would complain. I would
Love you ten years before the Flood,
And you should, if you please, refuse
Till the conversion of the Jews;
My vegetable Love should grow
Vaster than Empires and more slow;
An hundred years should go to praise
Thine Eyes, and on thy Forehead Gaze;
Two hundred to adore each Breast,
But thirty thousand to the rest;
An Age at least to every part,
And the last Age should show your Heart.
For, Lady, you deserve this State,
Nor would I love at lower rate.
   But at my back I alwaies hear
Times wingèd Charriot hurrying near:
And yonder all before us lye
Deserts of vast Eternity.
Thy Beauty shall no more be found;
Nor, in thy marble Vault, shall sound
My ecchoing Song; then Worms shall try
That long-preserve'd Virginity:
And your quaint Honour turn to dust;

And into ashes all my Lust.
The Grave's a fine and private place,
But none, I think, do there embrace.
   Now therefore, while the youthful hew
Sits on thy skin like morning dew,
And while thy willing Soul transpires
At every pore with instant Fires,
Now let us sport us while we may;
And now, like am'rous birds of prey,
Rather at once our Time devour,
Than languish in his slow-chapt pow'r.
Let us roll all our Strength, and all
Our sweetness, up into one Ball,
And tear our Pleasures with rough strife,
Thorough the Iron gates of Life.
Thus, though we cannot make our Sun
Stand still, yet we will make him run.

Epitaph

Enough: and leave the rest to Fame;
'Tis to commend her, but to name.
Courtship which, living, she declined,
When dead, to offer were unkind:
Where never any could speak ill
Who would officious praises spill?
Nor can the truest wit or friend,
Without detracting, her commend.
To say she lived a virgin chaste
In this age loose and all unlaced;
Nor was, when Vice is so allowed,
Of Virtue or ashamed, or proud;
That her soul was on Heaven so bent,
No minute but it came and went:
That, ready her last debt to pay,
She summed her life up every day;
Modest as morn; as mid-day bright,
Gentle as evening; cool as night;
'Tis true; but all too weakly said;
'Twas more significant, she's dead.

HENRY VAUGHAN
1621–95

Peace

My Soul, there is a Countrie
   Far beyond the stars,
Where stands a winged sentrie
   All skilfull in the wars,
There above noise, and danger
   Sweet Peace sits crown'd with smiles,
And one born in a Manger
   Commands the Beauteous files,
He is thy gracious friend,
   And (O my Soul awake!)
Did in pure love descend
   To die here for thy sake;
If thou canst get but thither,
   There growes the flowre of peace,
The Rose that cannot wither,
   Thy fortresse, and thy ease;
Leave then thy foolish ranges;
   For none can thee secure,
But one, who never changes,
   Thy God, thy life, thy Cure.

The Retreate

Happy those early dayes! when I
Shin'd in my Angell-infancy.
Before I understood this place
Appointed for my second race,
Or taught my soul to fancy ought
But a white, Celestiall thought,
When yet I had not walkt above

A mile, or two, from my first love,
And looking back (at that short space,)
Could see a glimpse of his bright-face;
When on some gilded Cloud, or flowre
My gazing soul would dwell an houre,
And in those weaker glories spy
Some shadows of eternity;
Before I taught my tongue to wound
My Conscience with a sinfull sound,
Or had the black art to dispense
A sev'rall sinne to ev'ry sense,
But felt through all this fleshly dresse
Bright shootes of everlastingnesse.
   O how I long to travell back
And tread again that ancient track!
That I might once more reach that plaine,
Where first I left my glorious traine,
From whence th' Inlightned spirit sees
That shady City of Palme trees;
But (ah!) my soul with too much stay
Is drunk, and staggers in the way.
Some men a forward motion love,
But I by backward steps would move,
And when this dust falls to the urn
In that state I came return.

The World

I saw Eternity the other night
Like a great Ring of pure and endless light,
   All calm, as it was bright,
And round beneath it, Time in hours, days, years
      Driv'n by the spheres
Like a vast shadow mov'd, In which the world
   And all her train were hurl'd;
The doting Lover in his queintest strain
      Did there Complain,

Neer him, his Lute, his fancy, and his flights,
    Wits sour delights,
With gloves, and knots the silly snares of pleasure;
    Yet his dear Treasure
All scatter'd lay, while he his eyes did pour
    Upon a flowr.

The darksome States-man, hung with weights and woe,
Like a thick midnight-fog mov'd there so slow
    He did nor stay, nor go;
Condemning thoughts (like sad Ecclipses) scowl
        Upon his soul,
And Clouds of crying witnesses without
    Pursued him with one shout.
Yet digg'd the Mole, and lest his ways be found
        Workt under ground,
Where he did Clutch his prey, but one did see
        That policie;
Churches and altars fed him, Perjuries
    Were gnats and flies,
It rain'd about him blood and tears, but he
        Drank them as free.

The fearfull miser on a heap of rust
Sate pining all his life there, did scarce trust
    His own hands with the dust,
Yet would not place one peece above, but lives
        In feare of theeves.
Thousands there were as frantick as himself
        And hugg'd each one his pelf,
The down-right Epicure plac'd heav'n in sense
        And scornd pretence
While others slipt into a wide Excesse
        Said little lesse;
 The weaker sort slight, triviall wares inslave
        Who think them brave,
And poor, despised truth sate Counting by
        Their victory.

Yet some, who all this while did weep and sing,
And sing, and weep, soar'd up into the Ring,
    But most would use no wing.
O fools (said I,) thus to prefer dark night
        Before true light,
To live in grots, and caves, and hate the day
        Because it shews the way,
The way which from this dead and dark abode
        Leads up to God,
A way where you might tread the Sun, and be
        More bright than he.
But as I did their madness so discusse
        One whisper'd thus,
This Ring the Bride-groome did for none provide
        But for his bride.

JOHN 2: 16–17

All that is in the world, the lust of the flesh, the lust of the eyes,
    and the pride of life, is not of the father, but is of the world.
And the world passeth away, and the lusts thereof, but he that
    doth the will of God abideth for ever.

Quickness

False life! a foil and no more, when
        Wilt thou be gone?
Thou foul deception of all men
That would not have the true come on.

Thou art a moon-like toil; a blind
        Self-posing state
A dark contest of waves and wind;
A mere tempestuous debate.

Life is a fixed discerning light,
        A knowing joy;
 No chance, or fit: but ever bright,
And calm and full, yet doth not cloy.

'Tis such a blissful thing, that still
        Doth vivify!
And shine and smile, and hath the skill
To please without Eternity.

Thou art a toilsome mole, or less,
        A moving mist;
But life is, what none can express,
A quickness which my God hath kissed.

The Dwelling-Place

What happy, secret fountain,
Fair shade, or mountain,
Whose undiscover'd virgin glory
Boasts it this day, though not in story,
Was then thy dwelling? did some cloud
Fix'd to a Tent, descend and shroud
My distrest Lord? or did a star
Beckon'd by thee, though high and far,
In sparkling smiles haste gladly down
To lodge light, and increase her own?

My dear, dear God! I do not know
What lodg'd thee then, nor where, nor how;
But I am sure, thou dost now come
Oft to a narrow, homely room,
Where thou too hast but the least part,
My God, I mean *my sinful heart*.

JOHN 1: 38–9

Then Jesus turned, and saw them following, and saith unto them, what seek ye? They said unto him, Rabbi (which is to say, being interpreted, Master), where dwellest thou? He saith unto them, Come and see. They came and saw where he dwelt, and abode with him that day: for it was about the tenth hour.

THOMAS TRAHERNE
1638–74

News

News from a foreign country came,
As if my treasure and my wealth lay there:
So much it did my heart enflame,
'Twas wont to call my soul into mine ear,
   Which thither went to meet
      The approaching sweet,
And on the threshold stood,
To entertain the unknown Good.
      It hovered there
   As if 'twould leave mine ear,
   And was so eager to embrace
The joyful tidings as they came,
'Twould almost leave its dwelling place,
      To entertain that same.

As if the tidings were the things,
My very joys themselves, my foreign treasure –
   Or else did bear them on their wings –
With so much joy they came, with so much pleasure
   My soul stood at that gate
To recreate
   Itself with bliss, and to
Be pleased with speed. A fuller view
   It fain would take,
   Yet journeys back would make
Unto my heart: as if 'twould fain
   Go out to meet, yet stay within
   To fit a place to entertain,
      And bring the tidings in.

   What sacred instinct did inspire
   My soul in childhood with a hope so strong?
   What sacred force moved my desire

To expect my joys beyond the seas, so young?
    Felicity I knew
    Was out of view;
  And being here alone,
I saw that happiness was gone
    From me! For this,
    I thirsted absent bliss,
And thought that sure beyond the seas,
  Or else in something near at hand –
I knew not yet – since nought did please
I knew – my bliss did stand.

But little did the infant dream
That all the treasures of the world were by;
  And that himself was so the cream
And crown of all which round about did lie.
  Yet thus it was: the gem,
        The diadem,
      The ring enclosing all
    That stood upon this earthly ball,
        The Heavenly eye,
    Much wider than the sky,
Wherein they all included were,
  The glorious Soul, that was the King
Made to possess them, did appear
    A small and little thing!

JOHN WILMOT,
EARL OF ROCHESTER
1647–80

A Song of a Young Lady.
To her Ancient Lover

Ancient Person, for whom I,
All the flattering Youth defy;
Long be it e're thou grow Old,
Aking, shaking, Crazy Cold.
But still continue as thou art,
Ancient Person of my Heart.

On thy wither'd Lips and dry,
Which like barren Furrows lye,
Brooding Kisses I will pour,
Shall thy Youthful Heat restore.
Such kind Show'rs in Autumn fall,
And a second Spring recall:
Nor from thee will ever part,
Ancient Person of my Heart.

Thy Nobler parts, which but to name
In our Sex would be counted shame,
By Ages frozen grasp possest,
From their Ice shall be releast:
And sooth'd by my reviving hand,
In former Warmth and Vigor stand.
All a Lover's wish can reach,
For thy Joy my Love shall teach:
And for thy Pleasure shall improve,
All that Art can add to Love.
Yet still I love thee without Art,
Ancient Person of my Heart.

Love and Life. A Song

All my past Life is mine no more,
   The flying Hours are gone:
Like transitory Dreams giv'n o'er,
Whose Images are kept in store
   By Memory alone.

The Time that is to come is not;
   How can it then be mine?
The present Moment's all my Lot;
And that, as fast as it is got,
   Phillis, is only thine.

Then talk not of Inconstancy,
   False Hearts, and broken Vows;
If I, by Miracle, can be
This live-long Minute true to thee,
   'Tis all that Heav'n allows.

BIOGRAPHIES

Sir Walter Raleigh (1552?–1618) was an adventurer, explorer, historian, naval commander, poet and statesman who came from an old Devon family. A favourite of Queen Elizabeth I, he fell from favour following Elizabeth's death in 1603 and James I had him beheaded on Tower Hill on 29 October 1618. His poetry has survived as a fitting memorial to this remarkable, noble, gallant and polymathical man who managed to exercise his many talents in a golden age of English life and expansion.

William Shakespeare (1564–1616) was the son of a prosperous merchant of Stratford-upon-Avon. He was almost certainly educated at the local grammar school, but did not attend university. According to John Aubrey, his early career was spent as a country schoolmaster, and it is known that he was established as a playwright by 1592. He married Anne Hathaway in 1582 and they had two daughters and a son. He died on 23 April 1616 and is buried in Holy Trinity Church, Stratford. His genius as a dramatist and poet defies superlatives.

Sir Henry Wotton (1568–1639) was born in Kent and educated at Winchester and New College and The Queen's College, Oxford, before entering the Middle Temple. He became secretary to the Earl of Essex and travelled abroad extensively on diplomatic missions. He became Provost of Eton in 1624.

John Donne (1572–1631) was the son of a wealthy ironmonger. At Oxford he formed what was to be a lifelong friendship with Sir Henry Wotton. In 1601 he secretly married Ann Moore, the seventeen-year-old niece of his employer, Sir Thomas Egerton, for which social solecism he was briefly imprisoned when the union was discovered in 1602. He and Ann subsequently had twelve children of whom seven survived. Brought up as a Roman Catholic, he later joined the Church of England. He took Holy Orders in 1615 and became a royal chaplain and a reader in divinity at Lincoln's Inn before becoming Dean of St Paul's in 1621. A popular and remarkable preacher, he also wrote much respected and enduring verse in the form of elegies, epigrams, religious pieces and satires, and he is widely regarded as the greatest of the metaphysical poets.

Ben Jonson (1573?–1637) was born of Scottish descent in Westminster and attended Westminster School. He first worked as a bricklayer and then spent some time as a soldier before becoming an actor and a playwright. He published two collections of poems, *The Forest* (1616) and *Underwoods* (1640). He was the *de facto* Poet Laureate of his day. He is buried in Westminster Abbey.

Edward, Lord Herbert of Cherbury (1583–1648) was born in Shropshire, his father being the sheriff of Montgomeryshire. He was the elder brother of George Herbert (see below). He married at sixteen while at University College, Oxford. He was knighted by James I at his coronation in 1603, and was advanced to an Irish peerage in 1624 and to an English barony in 1629. A supporter of the Royalist cause in the English Civil War, he nevertheless subsequently made his peace with Parliament. He is the author of both metaphysical prose and verse of note.

Henry King (1592–1669) was the son of a Bishop of London. He was educated at Westminster School and Christ Church, Oxford. He took Holy Orders and became Bishop of Chichester in 1642. He wrote elegies on royalty and on his friends, who included John Donne, Ben Jonson and Izaak Walton.

Francis Quarles (1592–1644) was born near Romford, Essex, the son of a surveyor-general of victualling for the Navy. He was educated at Christ's College, Cambridge, and subsequently entered Lincoln's Inn to study law. He married twice and had eighteen children, all by his first wife. He sided with the Royalists in the English Civil War and it is said that the removal and destruction of his books by the victorious Parliamentary Party broke his heart and brought about his death.

George Herbert (1593–1633), the brother of Lord Herbert of Cherbury (see above), was educated at Westminster School and Trinity College, Cambridge. He was a friend of Francis Bacon, John Donne and Sir Henry Wotton (see above). After a time at the court of James I, he took Holy Orders in 1626 and became Rector of Bemerton in Wiltshire in 1630, where he wrote his very highly regarded religious verse. He was also a classical scholar of note and an accomplished musician.

Thomas Carew (1595–1640) was the son of a lawyer. He was educated at Oxford University and studied law at the Inner Temple. His poetry was written about the life of the court and gallantry, and it is popular for its beauty, grace and tenderness.

Sir William Davenant (1606–68) was the son of the landlord of the Crown Inn in the Cornmarket, Oxford, whose tavern was frequently visited by Shakespeare, his godfather. He was educated at grammar school in Oxford and entered the service of Lord Brooke. Siding with the Royalists in the English Civil War, he was imprisoned but escaped to France and was knighted by Charles I on his return to England. He was imprisoned in the Tower again from 1650–2 being released through the good offices of John Milton. He was imprisoned again in 1659, but was restored to favour at the Restoration.

Edmund Waller (1606–87) was born into a wealthy Buckinghamshire family and educated at Eton and King's College, Cambridge. He studied law at Lincoln's Inn and became a Member of Parliament at the age of sixteen. He consolidated his considerable fortune by marrying Anne Banks, an heiress, in 1631. She died in 1634 and he subsequently sought, unsuccessfully, to gain the hand of Lady Dorothea Sidney who inspired some of his most memorable poems. He was disgraced by Parliament during the English Civil War, but managed by numerous twists and turns to restore himself to favour and his seat in Parliament on the Restoration.

John Milton (1608–74) was born in London, the son of a scrivener (scribe) of yeoman stock. He was educated at St Paul's School and Christ's College, Cambridge, where his rare beauty led to his being referred to as 'The Maid of Christ's'. Thrice married (his first two wives died), Milton became Foreign Secretary to the Council of State under the Commonwealth, in which post he was assisted by Andrew Marvell. He was pardoned at the Restoration due to the intercession of Davenant (see above) and Marvell on his behalf. He died blind and plagued by gout and he lies buried in St Giles, Cripplegate.

Sir John Suckling (1609–42) was the son of a knight. He was born at Twickenham, Middlesex, and educated at Trinity College, Cambridge, subsequently entering Gray's Inn to study law. He came into a large inheritance on the death of his father in 1627 and became a favourite at the court of Charles I, by whom he was knighted. He was forced to flee from England over his involvement in a plot to rescue Stafford from the Tower of London, and is reputed to have committed suicide in Paris. A famous gambler he was the inventor of the game of cribbage.

Richard Crashaw (1612?–49) was the son of a clergyman and was educated at Charterhouse and Pembroke College, Cambridge. He was ejected as a Fellow of Peterhouse, Cambridge, for refusing to accept the Solemn League and Covenant. He travelled to Europe, became a Roman Catholic and occupied various ecclesiastical posts. He is commemorated in a charming ode by his friend, Abraham Cowley (see below).

Abraham Cowley (1618–67) was the son of a wealthy London stationer. A precociously bright child, he was educated at Westminster School and Trinity College, Cambridge. He was a devoted Royalist and served the cause abroad during the English Civil War, but was disappointed with what he took to be his meagre reward at the Restoration. He is reputed by Pope to have died as a result of a fever contracted by lying out in the open after a heavy drinking session. He is buried in Westminster Abbey near to Spenser, who was the source of much of his inspiration.

Richard Lovelace (1618–58) was the son of a wealthy Kentish knight, Sir William Lovelace. He was born at Woolwich and educated at Charterhouse and Gloucester Hall, Oxford. An ardent Royalist, he dissipated a fortune in that cause and died in poverty. Like many writers of his age, much of his work was undertaken while in prison.

Andrew Marvell (1621–78), the son of a clergyman, was born in Yorkshire. He was educated at Hull Grammar School and Trinity College, Cambridge. A popular and hard-working Member of Parliament for Hull he held strong republican sympathies, but was held in high regard by Charles II. He wrote many satires, but is best remembered for his poetry which, although not extensive, is of a very high standard.

Henry Vaughan (1621–95), a cousin of John Aubrey, was born in Brecknockshire and educated at Jesus College, Oxford. He studied law in London but became a physician in Brecon and Newton-by-Usk. Following a serious illness, almost all his writing was on a religious theme. His short but exquisite poem 'The Retreat' inspired Wordsworth to write his 'Ode on the Intimations of Immortality'.

Thomas Traherne (1638–74) was born in Hereford, the son of a shoemaker. He was educated at Brasenose College, Oxford, and took Holy Orders in 1657. He became chaplain to Sir Orlando Bridgeman, Lord Keeper of the Great Seal, in 1667. His poems were discovered in manuscript form on a bookstall in 1896. At first thought to be the work of Vaughan (see above), they were correctly identified by Bertram Dobell and published in 1903.

John Wilmot, 2nd Earl of Rochester (1647–80), was born at Ditchley, Oxfordshire, and was educated briefly at Wadham College, Oxford, becoming an MA at fourteen. Charming, handsome and witty he was a brave, swashbuckling character who saw active service in the Dutch War and became a notoriously dissolute and libertine member of Charles II's court. He died, exhausted from self-indulgence, alcoholism and venereal disease, at the age of thirty-three, having embraced Christianity in the closing months of his life, leaving a legacy of some exquisite verse which although often suppressed has stood the test of time.

INDEX OF POEM TITLES

INDEX OF POEM FIRST LINES

Gaze not on thy beauties pride 77
Give me more love, or more disdain 81
Give me my Scallop shell of quiet 3
Goe, and catche a falling starre 16
Goe lovely Rose 88
Great heart, who taught thee so to dye ? 5

Had we but World enough, and Time 108
Happy those early dayes! when I 110
Having been tenant long to a rich Lord 58
Heare mee, O God! 44
Here take my Picture; though I bid farewell 9
How should I praise Thee, Lord ? how should my rymes 64
How soon doth man decay! 70

I got me flowers to straw Thy way 59
I had preparèd many a flowre 60
I know the wayes of Learning; both the head 68
I long to talke with some old lovers ghost 31
I made a posie while the day ran by 69
I saw Eternity the other night 111
I scarce beleeve my love to be so pure 22
I struck the board, and cry'd, 'No more 71
I was foretold, your rebell sex 82
I wonder by my troth, what thou, and I 15
If poysonous mineralls, and if that tree 37
In what torne ship soever I embarke 41
It is not that I love you less 87
It was the Winter wilde 91

Know Celia, (since thou art so proud,) 83

Let mans Soule be a Spheare, and then, in this 40
Let me powre forth 24
Like to the falling of a Starre 53
Lord, what is Man ? why should he cost Thee 101
Lord, Who createdst man in wealth and store 61
Love bade me welcome; yet my soul drew back 76

Mark how the bashful morn in vain 83

Marke but this flea, and marke in this 14
Must I then see, alas! eternal night 46
My mistress' eyes are nothing like the sun 6
My once dear Love! hapless that I no more 53
My Soul, there is a Countrie 110

News from a foreign country came 115
No, no, fair Heretick, it needs must be 100
Now you have freely given me leave to love 85

Oh my blacke Soule! now thou art summoned 36
Oh thou great Power, in whom I move, 7
Oh! for some honest Lovers ghost 98
Our storme is past, and that storms tyrannous rage 12
Out upon it, I have lov'd 99

Prayer, the Churche's banquet, Angels' age 65

Rise, heart, Thy Lord is risen; sing His praise 59

Since I am comming to that Holy roome 42
Since she whom I lov'd hath payd her last debt 39
So, so, breake off this last lamenting kisse 34
Some that have deeper digg'd loves Myne then I 25
Spit in my face you Jewes, and pierce my side 38
Still to be neat, still to be drest 45
Sweetest love, I do not goe 19

Teach me, my God and King 75
Tell me no more how fair she is 49
Tell me not (Sweet) I am unkinde 105
The fleet astronomer can bore 67
The lark now leaves his wat'ry nest 86
The Thirsty Earth soaks up the Rain 104
This is the Month, and this the happy morn 90
Thou hast made me, And shall thy worke decay? 35
Throw away Thy rod 73
'Tis the yeares midnight, and it is the dayes 26
To these, whom Death again did wed 103
Twice or thrice had I loved thee 20